endorsements

"In a time when most followers of Jesus consume or criticize culture, Brett Ullman does neither. Rather, he thoughtfully creates and critiques culture. In Brett's most recent project—*media.faith.culture*—his heart and mind come through clear as he strategically navigates readers through the complex media maze."

—**Kary Oberbrunner**
Founder of Redeem the Day, Pastor, and Author
of *Your Secret Name* and *The Fine Line*
www.karyoberbrunner.com

"Engaging culture with a Christian worldview is something of an art, but Brett does it in such a down-to-earth and welcomed way. His approach of enabling students to come up with their own conscious and healthy decisions towards media is so important and needed. The moment we as parents, youth leaders, and mentors disengage from discussions on media and culture is the moment our students will begin interpreting these mediums in unhealthy ways. Sheltering students should never be the approach taken and Brett provides his readers with the criteria by which we engage in constructive conversation."

—Matt Naismith
Student Ministries Teaching and Leadership Pastor Lakeside Church, Guelph
www.lakesidechurch.ca

"Brett is a fantastic communicator and his new book does not disappoint. Brett points out the Giant Elephant in the Room, the one we know is there but never want to discuss, with great clarity and passion. This book is well-sourced and as a pastor and parent I am challenged even deeper to engage in these difficult conversations. I recommend this book as a must-read."

—Don Bennett
Associate Pastor, The Meeting House, Oakville
www.themeetinghouse.ca

"Our choices determine our future. Brett Ullman has dedicated himself to helping both youth and parents seek our positive influences while guarding themselves from things that can destroy them. This book is a powerful tool that every leader, minister, and parent needs to read. It will both help them understand the issues this generation faces and to prepare our youth to make the right choices."

—David Sawler
Pastor, Speaker, and Author
of *Goodbye Generation* and *The Disciple*
www.davidsawler.com

"I have yet to come across a book dealing with media, faith and culture that not only challenges your view on these three issues but calls you to put into practice what you've read and offers practical ways of applying that challenge to everyday life—until now. Brett Ullman has done an excellent job in not only addressing the issues of media, faith, and culture but also providing tools for one to act on what they've read... making this not just theoretical book but a very practical one! A definite must read... not just for youth and young adults but parents and leaders as well!"

—**Dwayne Hutchings**
Creative Ministries Pastor, The Gathering Place
www.pickeringpentecostal.com

"Brett is one of the most skilled and current communicators I know. I've had the opportunity to share many events with Brett, and I am constantly challenged by what he has to say about media, faith, and culture. This book does a great job of representing where we are at as a society and culture today, and is a must-read for anybody seeking to live out our faith in our modern world."

—**Josh McCabe**
Nine O Five Visionary
www.nineofive.ca

media.faith.culture

Brett Ullman

Worlds Apart Series - Book 1

media.faith.culture

Printed in Canada.

Word Alive Press
131 Cordite Road, Winnipeg, MB R3W 1S1
www.wordalivepress.ca

Library and Archives Canada Cataloguing in Publication

Ullman, Brett, 1971-
Media, faith, culture : connecting our ancient faith with our modern world / Brett Ullman.

(World's apart ; bk. 1)
ISBN 978-1-77069-140-7

1. Christianity and culture. 2. Mass media--Influence. 3. Mass media--Religious aspects--Christianity. 4. Technology--Religious aspects--Christianity. 5. Popular culture--Religious aspects--Christianity. I. Title. II. Series: Ullman, Brett, 1971- . World's apart ; bk. 1.

BR115.C8U55 2010 261.5'2 C2010-907225-1

To all my fellow journeyers who are living life trying to connect their ancient faith to their modern world.

acknowledgements

Thanks to my wife Dawn and my children Zoe and Bennett for all their support over the years with the work I do at Worlds Apart. Thanks to Adam Clarke for his dedication and hard work on this project. Thanks to all my Board of Directors, both past (Daniel McKay, Dave Crawford, Scott Trowbridge, James Boyle, Neil Pasher, Rick Britnell) and present (Brian Althouse, Peter Bozanis, James Cabral, Doug Gowdy, Brian Hall, Andrew Malloch, Brian McAuley, Todd Skinner), for helping behind the scenes. I would like to also thank the other people who have been an integral part of the work at Worlds Apart: Geoff and Erin Thompson (3rdglance.com), Jeff Smyth, Caroline Bruckner, Gary Powell, Tracey Paris and many others. I would also like to thank the people who have supported us through prayer and financial support. We could not do this without you.

I would also like to thank my sponsors who support the work that I do. Thanks to Tyndale University, College and

Seminary (Tyndale.ca), World Vision (worldvision.ca), Carruthers Creek Community Church (carrutherscreek.ca), Interlinc (interlinc-online.com)

introduction

"There is perhaps nothing worse than reaching the top of the ladder and discovering that you're on the wrong wall."[1]

I think many of us can relate to reaching the top of a ladder, only to discover we are in the wrong place. How is it so simple for us to end up where we never thought we would be? Many times we realize this when it is too late, too late to turn back and make some well-managed changes so that we can reach the right heights for our lives. None of us have arrived. If you think your best years are going to be in high school, I feel sorry for you. We should always strive and believe that our lives will improve and get

---

[1] Soccio, Douglas J. *Archetypes of Wisdom: An Introduction to Philosophy*, 7th Edition (Belmont, CA: Wadsworth Publishing, 2009), p. 153.

better as we move forward and grow through new experiences.

I hope no one begins reading this book thinking they are at the top of their ladder, at the peak of their existence, having arrived at perfection. Simply put, that just isn't the case with any of us. But worse than that would be approaching this book with the thought that you can't change. I hope you don't think you have climbed so high that there is no way to scale back down without hurling yourself off the ladder. That isn't the case, either. We can journey together—a journey of questions and respectable conversation. I hope we can all come in with the mindset that something could change.

Here is the biggest struggle with writing this book: what could I say to make you change anything?

If all I do is write this book, or if I have the opportunity to speak in front of you for a few hours and that's it, what a waste of time writing this book will have been. I'll give you everything I have; all I ask of you is that you allow your heart, mind, and soul to be open to the possibility of change, and more importantly to question.

What should we question? That seems like a perfect place to start because the answer gives us an infinite number of possibilities. We should allow ourselves to question everything around us. Whether it is TV, magazines, movies, or the music we listen to, we should always be asking questions.

What values does the author have?

What do the lyrics say is normal?

Will that t-shirt really change the way people treat me?

These are all questions that will lead us into a world that is conscious of the messages that are all around us every day. Without the possibility of asking questions, the world would be a very boring place with very boring people who only believe what they are told to believe.

What are these messages that we hear all around us?

It's noise! It is the noise that comes from the constant messages being fired at us through our phones, emails, texts, and the many screens that exist in our lives. The noisy messages that are making up our choices, values, and belief systems allow us to do one thing very well—hide. We can hide behind our screens and enter a world that seems enticing and perfect, but it only appears this way because we haven't begun to question what this noise has done to our lives.

What do you consciously hide from your parents?

Is it your music, what you watch on TV and on the Internet, or is it everything you possibly can?

Why do you hide behind these screens? If it is a feeling of guilt, we are on the right track. That feeling of uncertainty you have while watching or listening is an internal questioning already at work. That awkward feeling in the pit of your stomach is sometimes the coolest part of change, because it happens without our knowledge or probing. It just happens.

Why does it happen?

It happens because something you have just read, watched, or listened to does not agree with what you have determined to be true, noble, or genuinely good. That is why when we see violence happen in a movie we have the same feeling in the pit of our stomach as when we see it close to home. We know that it (violence, greed, excessive swearing, etc.) is not a part of an everyday, normal life. As we begin to question and probe all the noise and screens in our lives, we begin to make clearer choices on what we allow to influence us.

table of contents

MEDIA

media

Let's dive into the media, or the noise that is bombarding us every day. A recent study done by the Kaiser Foundation, called *Generation M2: Media in the Lives of 8- to 18-Year-Olds*, reported the following numbers about the amount of media found in the average household.

> Today the typical 8- to 18-year-old's home contains an average of 3.8 TVs, 2.8 DVD or VCR players, 1 digital video recorder, 2.2 CD players, 2.5 radios, 2 computers, and 2.3 console video game players. Except for radios and CD players, there has been a steady increase in the number of media platforms in young people's homes over the past 10 years (with the advent of the MP3 player, the number of radios and CD players has actually declined in recent years).[2]

---

[2] Rideout, Victoria J., Ulla G. Foehr, Donald F. Roberts and Henry J. Kaiser Family Foundation, *Generation M2: Media in the Lives of 8- to 18-Year-Olds* (Menlo Park, CA: Henry J. Kaiser Family Foundation, 2010).

There was also a huge increase in the amount of time spent enjoying one form of media or another.

> Moreover, given the amount of time they spend using more than one medium at a time, today's youth pack a total of 10 hours and 45 minutes worth of media content into those daily 7½ hours—an increase of almost 2¼ hours of media exposure per day over the past five years.[3]

So, we have a couple of issues that we need to address.

1) There is more media devices in your life than there was in mine, and
2) You spend on average two more hours a day engaged in media than my generation did.

What does media mean to you? What is the first thing you think of when you hear the word "media"?

Media is defined by the author David Dark as the "plural for the mediums through which someone or something is getting through (or trying to get through) to us. Let's name a few: letters, billboards, cell phones, novels, songs, newspapers, magazines, television, and emails."[4] I would add video games and movies to that list as well. Media by its very definition is communication, and that is where our questioning begins. We need to question what is being

---

[3] Ibid.

[4] Dark, David. *The Sacredness of Questioning Everything* (Grand Rapids, MI: Zondervan, 2009), pp. 95-96.

communicated to us, who is doing the communicating, and what we are communicating back from what we hear. In other words, how is what we are influenced by influencing those around us?

Let me tell you a story of my first experience with media and its influence.

I was seventeen and I can honestly say this day would turn out to be one of the weirdest days of my life. I was going with my youth group to hear a media talk, much similar to what this book is doing… or at least I thought that's what the night was going to be. Next thing I knew, a man came into the room with some records (you know, the big version of CDs) and played them backwards… all night long. That was it. That was his means of getting his message across to us.

That wasn't the weird part. The weird part came when he finally spoke. He asked us four simple words—"Did you hear that?"

He didn't tell us to listen for anything before he finally came around to speak, and when he did speak no one knew what he was talking about. Instead of a response, he received blank stares and looks of confusion from everyone in the room.

Finally, he told us what we heard—at least, what we were *supposed* to hear. Here is how the next couple of minutes played out.

"It says, go worship Satan," he said.

I said, "Dude, no, it doesn't."

"Yes, it does."

With the simple answer of "Yes, it does," his point was apparently made and he could move on to the next record. No questioning of the message was allowed, and thus he proved his point, I guess. "Go have sex" was the apparent message of the next backward record, and that was my first experience with media, its influence and message, and how it apparently affects our lives.

Are we tired of being told what media is saying?

At the end of the night, he was convinced that he had made his point, to which I still said, "No, you didn't." What was his message that night? Christians should not listen to any secular music. To be very honest and blunt, I disagree with the term "secular music," and I completely disagree with the term "Christian music." That night, I was not just told who I could or couldn't listen to, but I was handed a record that was acceptable in his eyes for me to listen to. It was a record by Sandy Patty, and if anyone under the age of twenty-five knows who I'm talking about I'll be surprised. The record was, in his view, good old Christian music that would not lead me astray. Now, my favourite band growing up was Skinny Puppy, a band that had lyrics ripe with language. They were a far cry from the Sandy Patty record that had just been placed in my hand.

I look back and think it was funny, but back then it was far from funny. I took that record with me to the bus, but it did not make the journey back home with me; I smashed it on the ground beside the bus. That night held some very severe consequences for my personal relationship with Jesus. The Jesus presented to me that night was not a Jesus I wanted any part of and I did not want to go back. Many times we are presented with a Jesus who is far from the Jesus that truly is. As a young kid, the church—and this false presentation of who God was—turned me off, and it should not have been that way. The reality of the situation is that the Jesus we preach is not always the Jesus who is.

There is a danger when we begin to label things Christian and secular. Rob Bell, in his book *Velvet Elvis*, responds to our tendency to label things secular and Christian by pointing out that if we begin to label the messages coming at us we lose sight of what is acceptable.

> The danger of labeling things 'Christian' is that it can lead to our blindly consuming things we have been told are safe and acceptable. When we turn off this discernment radar, dangerous things can happen. We have to test everything. I thank God for the many Christians who create and write and film and sing. Anybody anywhere who is doing all they can to point people to the deeper realities of God is doing a beautiful thing. But those writers and artists and thinkers and singers would all tell you to think long and hard about what they are saying and doing and creating. Test it. Probe it.[5]

Questioning the messages in our lives is not a new concept. Paul would have had to do the same as he travelled around Greece, learning about the pagan gods and engaging those within his community in conversation about what he

---

[5] Bell, Rob. *Velvet Elvis: Repainting the Christian Faith* (Grand Rapids, MI: Zondervan, 2005), p. 86.

read and learned along the way. Paul would not have believed or agreed with all the philosophers and poets he engaged with throughout Greece, but he questioned everything that was presented to him.

> In the same way that something can be labeled 'Christian' and not be true, something can be true and not be labeled Christian. Paul quotes Cretan prophets and Greek poets. He is interested in whether or not what they said is true. Now to be able to quote these prophets and poets, Paul obviously had to read them. And study them. And analyze them. And I'm sure he came across all kinds of things in their writings that he didn't agree with. So he sifts and sorts and separates the light from the dark and then claims and quotes parts that are true.[6]

This is my goal for this book, just as it is when I speak—question everything in your life and look for what has light and truth and what has darkness and lies. My goal, unlike the message I received as a teenager, is not to tell you what you should or should not listen to or watch at home, but simply a message of questioning. Allow yourself to question the messages that are coming at you, and then decide for yourself what you think the best and most truthful option would be.

---

[6] Ibid., p. 87.

Blind Lines

My first challenge is simple. Draw a black line in the space provided:

Okay, now look at your life. That's right, you just illustrated your life in, like, three seconds. It is that easy. This is what we do, though, isn't it? We draw a line in our life and say things like this: "I'll listen to this band, but not that band." How about this: "I'll watch this show, but not that show." We live a life that is separated by the lines we draw. When I ask why items are on one side of the line or another, the responses I hear are always interesting. They are interesting because we often don't know why, or we place them based on what others think or say or how they are perceived through media communication.

The line that confuses me and breaks my heart the most is the line we place in our church lives. We will team up with *this* church, but not *that* church. We exclude churches based on denominational titles, whether it is Baptist, Anglican, Pentecostal, or a community church. We refuse to work with the people down the street because of the title in their church name.

Have you ever had to read your Bible out loud in a group setting only to have someone look at you with disgust? I have, and it hurts. Why did this happen? Because I wasn't reading from the right translation, and this has happened many times and my response is always the same: "Well, would you like Greek, Hebrew, or both? What would you like?"

They all want the same thing—the good old King James Version (the one with the *thous* and the *thus sayith the LORDs*). But don't be discouraged. The Bible was not originally written in English and the same problems we have with one translation we have with another. All the English translations out there have been translated by humans from the original Greek and Hebrew sources.

Many teenagers have approached me with this same question: what version of the Bible should I read? Your parents might say English Standard Version (ESV), your pastor might be telling you to read New King James Version (NKJV), and your friends might be telling you to read The Voice translation because it is new, fresh, and easy to read. Quite often in our Christian circles we are asked to draw a thick line when it comes to the Bibles we read. I have some encouraging news for everyone out there. It does not have to be this way. I say read whatever translation, whatever Bible, you have and are comfortable reading.

I'll give you an example. There is a video on YouTube of a church in North Carolina that burned many versions of the Bible that were not the King James Version. They also burned many books by leading Christian authors because the church had clearly drawn some very thick and misguided lines when it came to the books they read. Representatives of this church said, "We are burning books that are satanic... Other Christian authors that we consider heretics, such as Billy Graham, Rick Warren..."[7]

The line that church is taking is that these books are okay over here, but those books in the pile are satanic and wrong. The problem is that they are labeling actual *Bibles* as having satanic influence in the world—Bibles such as the New International Version (NIV), The Message, the New King James Version (NKJV), and the American Standard Version (ASV), among others.

Does this line not go against the very nature and source of the Bible?

The Bible is God's word, given to us so that we can establish a relationship with him. The Bible is meant to show us how to gain everlasting life. The lines this North Carolina church is drawing says that certain Bibles don't tell the truth of God's word. The key word is *truth*.

Do you see the danger in drawing lines like that? It is easy to separate things into categories of right or wrong. We begin to separate things into categories so that we can then argue whether or not they are truly right or wrong.

In what areas do you separate things into categories?

I'll watch this show, but not that show.

I'll listen to this artist, but not that artist.

---

[7] Associated Press, *YouTube*, October 13, 2009, http://www.youtube.com/watch?v=4FkbgeR8LKs (accessed April 5, 2010).

I'll watch *Saw*, but I won't watch *Hostel*.

What do the categories say about what you value as right and wrong?

When we begin to separate things into categories, we usually end up with one of three worldviews based on how we see our role in the world.

The first, and quite honestly the easiest, choice is that we become separatists.[8] We remove ourselves completely from the world, people, society, and culture. The danger is not in the Christian bookstores, Christian camps, or religious schools because in and of themselves these things are not wrong. The problem is when we allow a separatist mindset to invade our whole life. The danger is in the message that is given to the world. Craig Gross and J.R. Mahon, in their book *Starving Jesus*, explain that the danger is that when we completely remove ourselves from culture and society without looking back, we are ignoring one of Jesus' core values. We no longer have the opportunity to teach the ways of Jesus to those who need it.

> Be in the world, not of it. We love to screw this one up. We automatically assume we should check out and pay no attention to the pop culture radar. Forget about people who are led astray. Build a bunker in the backyard, cover our kids' eyes and ears, and hope all your willpower and energy will be enough for the world to stay away. The problem with this behavior is when

[8] Oberbrunner, Kary. *The Journey Towards Relevance: Simple Steps for Transforming Your World* (Lake Mary, FL: Relevant Books, 2004).

> you follow Christ, you will be asked to serve those who are of the world.[9]

It is quite easy for us to look at the world around us and say that everything is bad, or even evil. That is an easy choice, because it takes no work at all; we just look around spotting everything that is against God and do nothing about it. This decision takes no effort or work on our part. God, however, tells us to avoid this type of worldview. *"Live creatively, friends. If someone falls into sin, forgivingly restore him, saving your critical comments for yourself. You might be needing forgiveness before the day's out"* (Galatians 6:1). In essence, God is saying, "Hey, live like me. I forgave, restored, and loved the people of this world, even though I am not of this world."

"And he said unto them, Ye are from beneath; I am from above: ye are of this world; I am not of this world" (John 8:23, KJV). Jesus had every right to live with a separatist view, because he did not sin; he was the only one who could look around at everyone around him and judge them by their sins.

One difference in our lives is pride. We overlook our own sins and judge others. We become too prideful to see our own sin when we condemn others. Here is what the Bible says about that: *"And why beholdest thou the mote that is in thy brother's eye, but considerest not the beam that is in thine own eye?"* (Matthew 7:3, KJV) We can also add this verse: *"If you live squinty-eyed in greed and distrust, your body is a*

---

[9] Gross, Craig and J.R. Mahon. *Starving Jesus: Off the Pew, Into the World* (Colorado Springs, CO: David C. Cook, 2007).

dank cellar. If you pull the blinds on your windows, what a dark life you will have!" (Matthew 6:23)

Do we notice the speck before the plank?

Jesus had to deal with this sort of thinking all the time in the form of Pharisees. They thought their law and commitment to the Torah (the Books of Moses) would keep them pure and holy. However, they were only separating themselves from everyone else through prideful arrogance. Jesus warned about this mentality in the Gospel of John: *"Ye search the scriptures, because ye think that in them ye have eternal life; and these are they which bear witness of me"* (John 5:39, ASV). In reality, it is easier to follow laws that are written down in a book, like the Ten Commandments, than to follow Jesus' ultimate commandment to love everyone.

> If all you do is love the lovable, do you expect a bonus? Anybody can do that. If you simply say hello to those who greet you, do you expect a medal? Any run-of-the-mill sinner does that. In a word, what I'm saying is, Grow up. You're kingdom subjects. Now live like it. Live out your God-created identity. Live generously and graciously toward others, the way God lives toward you. (Matthew 5:46–48)

Think about how Jesus treated the people of his time. He healed the sick, including the lepers who were outcasts. He sat with the woman at the well, he taught through the Samaritan, and he called the children to him. He loved without marginalizing. Jesus even tells us that oftentimes the world around us won't pollute our lives; it is how we let others influence our worldview. He then called the crowd together and said, *"Listen, and take this to heart. It's not what you swallow that pollutes your life, but what you vomit up"* (Matthew 15:10–11).

We have to ask questions about all the music, violence, and videos that come into our lives, because if we allow them to become our influences we become like the Pharisees. God, at that point, starts to fall away from the centre of our lives and media takes centre stage in guiding us, just as the Torah and other books of the law did for the Pharisees.

Pastor Chris Seay from Ecclesia Church in Houston recently said at a conference in Toronto that people and items—and in this case we can add media into the argument—should not be broken down into good and evil. He said that a better way to break these things down is in terms of shalom and not shalom. When we say things are straight-out evil, it conveys the message that the world is irreconcilable with God. God loses his power to reconcile and his authority is called into question. The cross loses its significance. However, if the person or object has "lost" shalom, it can be brought back to God and the grace of God is put into action.[10] When we start to live a separatist worldview, we begin seeing the world as irreconcilable—lost to God. The point we need to remember is that when we live in this worldview we take away the authority of God's word and places the authority on man's laws, which are flawed because of sin.

[10] Chris Seay, "Kingdom Economy Conference," in *Epiphaneia Network* (Toronto, ON: Epiphaneia Network Inc., 2010).

Our second choice is to become conformists. To conform is to give in to or submit to the rules or authority of something else. When we choose this route, unlike separatists, we turn to society, the world, and culture for all the answers.

Let me tell you about a friend of mine from university who really speaks about the danger of conforming. One day, we went to hang out, just like you are probably going to do later today, when he turned to me and said, "Brett, I want to start living my faith out among my people."

"Your people?" I responded.

At this point, I have come to understand that he is saying that his entire worldview has become an "Us vs. Them" issue. The great secular vs. Christian divide had shown up in his thoughts. The obstacle in this type of worldview is that the message and words of God can become diluted and, at times, lose their effectiveness.

He responded, "You know, bar people."

So he began going to the bar, sharing his faith when he could with people there, but he was quickly challenged on the Jesus he followed.

"Why would I need your Jesus?" one of his people challenged him. "You are exactly like me."

There is the danger of conforming completely to society and culture. Jesus in essence becomes just another homeboy (with the t-shirts and trucker hats) whose voice can be seen as a suggestion rather than the authoritative call to restoration it is supposed to be. This has become an issue for so many of us. We want the friendly, loving Jesus, but not the judge-and-jury Jesus. The moment we think our actions and thoughts are beyond judgment, we become unable to hear any criticism towards our own lives. It is the church and other believers who have the ability and calling to become accountability partners in our lives. However, we all know how we react to criticism and questions of accountability in our own lives. They are often reactions of self-preservation. We will say and do anything to keep those actions and thoughts justifiable and okay in our own minds.

Who do you have in your life to keep you accountable?

How do you react when they do their job?

Kary Oberbrunner explains why a conformist's attitude runs us into trouble:

> We want to escape laws, rules, and dead faith. But by alienating ourselves from communities of faith, we end up conforming to culture rather than transforming it. We set our sights on cruise control and feast on everything the world offers, not once thinking about what's tolerable and what's toxic.[11]

I think we have all gone through this at some point. We have all made a decision without thinking about the consequences. Conformists usually end up trying to please other people before they look to please God. I think my friend with his bar buddies went through this. His actions became so clouded with what was acceptable in that social scene that the actions and words of Jesus were lost.

---

[11] Oberbrunner, Kary. *The Fine Line: Re-envisioning the Gap Between Christ and Culture* (Grand Rapids, MI: Zondervan, 2008), p. 88.

How can we teach one worldview when we are trying to live out our social lives in another? That is a huge obstacle when it comes to living the worldview of a conformist. Conformists attempt to fix the appearance of unhip Christians who are against everything from movie theaters to music, but oftentimes they go too far in trying to show what they are for rather than what they are against. Many times, when trying to find what they can be for, the boundaries or views of the church frustrate conformists. Church, in their minds, becomes a place of order and rules and has no room for anything on the hip radar. They start to remove themselves from the larger church body, attempting to find ways to incorporate society and God without looking like church.

The book of Hebrews gives a strong warning against this removal from church:

> So let's do it—full of belief, confident that we're presentable inside and out. Let's keep a firm grip on the promises that keep us going. He always keeps his word. Let's see how inventive we can be in encouraging love and helping out, not avoiding worshiping together as some do but spurring each other on, especially as we see the big Day approaching. (Hebrews 10:22–25)

How can these words help us move away from a conformist worldview?

It is found in these words: *"Let's see how inventive we can be in encouraging love and helping out, not avoiding worshiping together..."* The key becomes creativity. Conformists seem to lack the sense that the term "creative Christians" is not an oxymoron. In God's autobiography, the first chapter would be called *He Creates All.* That was his first objective, and even as God was creating he was extremely creative, changing things up, moving one step at a time. He went from light to life, creating everything in seven days.

Creativity is a process that takes work. Conformists lack this understanding of the creative process. To them, church and religion become stale, and instead of working and using their creative forces to help out their communities, they walk away. Instead of walking away from the church in search of culture, we should try to engage culture in our church communities through prayer and understanding, so that our communities can stay informed and relevant. When we lose faith in the creativity of our churches, we leave in search of something new, something *hip*, something other than church and its rules, but when we rely on the cultural messages to guide us we can easily fall into idolatrous ways. Paul was well aware of this possibility and took initiative to warn his communities about this danger.

> The thing that has me so upset is that I care about you so much—this is the passion of God burning inside me! I promised your hand in marriage to Christ, presented you as a pure virgin to her husband. And now I'm afraid that exactly as the Snake seduced Eve with his smooth patter, you are being lured away from the simple purity of your love for Christ. It seems that if someone shows up preaching quite another Jesus than we preached—different spirit, different message—

> you put up with him quite nicely. (2 Corinthians 11:2–4)

Do we allow the false promises of culture to lure us away from church?

Do we really think culture has more answers than Christ?

There is a great warning about a conformist heart in 2 Timothy: *"You're going to find that there will be times when people will have no stomach for solid teaching, but will fill up on spiritual junk food—catchy opinions that tickle their fancy. They'll turn their backs on truth and chase mirages"* (2 Timothy 4:3–4). It is important that we remember that being Christian does not mean we have to lack creativity, because the moment we think that we have no creative output we start searching for other areas to become involved.

Jonathan Dodson came up with six ways to engage culture and one of the first ways he wrote about was through prayer.

> When engaging culture prayerfully, we depend on the wisdom that comes from the Spirit who searches out all cultures, who can enable us to recognize and rejoice in what is true, beautiful, and good, and reject or redeem what is false, ugly, and immoral. As a result, engaging culture can become an act of communion with God. Relying on the wisdom of the Spirit will also mean careful investigation of cultural issues, being criti-

> cal of our own biases while maintaining an open ear to the arguments of others.[12]

Conformists slowly begin to let the truth of God's word be replaced by the laissez-faire attitude of culture. Conformists lose their ability to go to God in silence and solitude because media becomes the guiding voice in their lives. The conformist camp, in search of freedom from rules and regulations, actually loses its creative force because it falls into the conformity of cultural norms and acceptance. They actually fall victim to the same rules they are running from. Lastly, they begin to tolerate instead of redeem.

Mad Men, a show that takes the audience into the lives of Madison Avenue ad men in the 1950s, portrays life through conformist eyes. The audience buys what they, the ad men, want us to buy. The consumer conforms his or her tastes in products to what people like Donald Draper tell us. In one scene, Rachel Menken, the owner of a high-class designer store, is in talks with Donald Draper about whether or not his agency should represent her store. She says, "Mr. Draper, I don't know what it is you really believe in, but I do know what it feels like to be out of place, to be disconnected, to see the whole world laid out in front of you the way other people live it. There is something about you that tells me you know it, too."[13] Conformists begin to see the world in that way. They want to live the way others

---

[12] Dodson, Jonathan. *Six Ways to Engage Culture*, http://theresurgence.com/Six_Ways_to_Engage_Culture (accessed April 5, 2010).

[13] Weiner, Matthew. *Mad Men: Smoke in Your Eyes*, Television Series, directed by Alan Taylor, 2007.

are living because they do not want to disturb the peace of everyone around them. Everything begins to look acceptable and mouldable to fit God's truth, but the reality is that, more often than not, idolatry is the result of this worldview.

The third choice we have is to be transformists. In *A Journey Toward Relevance,* author Kary Oberbrunner addresses a very important question we need to ask ourselves if we want to be agents of transformation in the world: how do I hold onto my cross when I reach out into the darkness?

> Integrating our faith with our culture can only happen if we have a faith to integrate! When our faith is shallow, our hopes of transforming culture are shallow. In order for an agent to transform something, it has to be different from it. Many of us are no different than the culture to begin with.[14]

In order to fully establish ourselves as possible transformists, we have to centre ourselves correctly. We must be holding onto our faith, but we also must be turning towards the world. The challenge with wanting to transform culture is that we need to gain a strong ability to listen to two voices at the same time.

Walt Mueller explains how and why it's important to gain the ability of double listening:

> ...the ability and resolve to listen to two voices at one time. He says that all Christians are called

---

[14] Oberbrunner, Kary. *The Journey Towards Relevence: Simple Steps for Transforming Your World* (Lake Mary, FL: Relevant Books, 2004), p. 127.

> to "stand between the Word and the world, with consequent obligation to listen to both. We listen to the Word in order to discover evermore of the riches of Christ. And we listen to the world in order to discern which of Christ's riches are needed most and how to present them in their best light." With our understanding of the Word and the world as a foundation, we can contextualize the gospel by sharing it in a meaningful way to the emerging generations.[15]

The Apostle Paul is an amazing example of someone who has this ability of double listening. In Acts, Paul goes to Athens and sits in its community places—an ancient-day Starbucks, if you will—and engages the people in philosophy, religion, life, and their gods. He listens to everything they have to say both for and against God and still calmly talks to them about the unknown statue in their midst.[16] Paul also has one of the best transformist stories imaginable. He went from being a Christian killer to a Christian defender and never took any credit for his transformation. In Philippians, Paul tells us about his transformed life.

> Steer clear of the barking dogs, those religious busybodies, all bark and no bite. All they're interested in is appearances—knife-happy circumcisers, I call them. The real believers are the ones

[15] Mueller, Walt. *Engaging the Soul of Youth Culture: Bridging Teen Worldviews and Christian Truth* (Downer's Grove, IL: InterVarsity Press, 2006), p. 51.

[16] Oberbrunner, Kary. *The Journey Towards Relevence: Simple Steps for Transforming Your World* (Lake Mary, FL: Relevant Books, 2004).

the Spirit of God leads to work away at this ministry, filling the air with Christ's praise as we do it. We couldn't carry this off by our own efforts, and we know it—even though we can list what many might think are impressive credentials. You know my pedigree: a legitimate birth, circumcised on the eighth day; an Israelite from the elite tribe of Benjamin; a strict and devout adherent to God's law; a fiery defender of the purity of my religion, even to the point of persecuting Christians; a meticulous observer of everything set down in God's law Book.

The very credentials these people are waving around as something special, I'm tearing up and throwing out with the trash—along with everything else I used to take credit for. And why? Because of Christ. Yes, all the things I once thought were so important are gone from my life. Compared to the high privilege of knowing Christ Jesus as my Master, firsthand, everything I once thought I had going for me is insignificant—dog dung. I've dumped it all in the trash so that I could embrace Christ and be embraced by him. I didn't want some petty, inferior brand of righteousness that comes from keeping a list of rules when I could get the robust kind that comes from trusting Christ—God's righteousness.

I gave up all that inferior stuff so I could know Christ personally, experience his resurrection power, be a partner in his suffering, and go all the way with him to death itself. If there was any way to get in on the resurrection from the dead, I wanted to do it. (Philippians 3:2–11)

Living a transformist life is quite often the hardest of the three choices because it takes a conscience choice to live it out. We have to decide to seek out the balance between knowledge of the word and the application of God's teaching. Too much of one leads to arrogance and too much of the other leads to a life rooted in the acceptance of everyone but Jesus. Like Paul, we need to make the choice between living like a separatist and acting like a conformist. Many times we choose to live out a combination of these lives—separatist, conformist, and transformist—all at the same time. It comes back to the question about the line.

1. When you get together with other Christians, what do you watch?
2. Do you watch nudity in films or on TV?
3. Do you listen to angry or abusive music?

Becoming a true tranformist needs to be a true commitment to a biblical worldview with no ands, ors, or buts. God requires our whole life to be a sacrifice, a temple dedicated to him, and it is an act of worship when we choose that solitary life.

It's a Sexy World Out There

Mark Sayers, in his book *The Vertical Self*, has noted a shift that has occurred in culture. The word "sexy" no longer appeals to just sexual attraction; it now gives something—or someone, in most cases—value. "When people in our culture attempt to act out being sexy, they are just trying to act in a way that makes them desirable to others—not necessarily as a sexual partner, but often just as a person others find interesting and valuable."[17] When we started labeling sport plays and meals sexy, we started down a slippery slope into a world that places value and worth on an allure and not actions and heart.

How many songs can you think of that promote the allure of sexiness?

"Sexy" now determines value, desirability, and status of power… and that means sex will be everywhere. From billboards to music videos, the cultural object now has to have a sexy vibe just so it can sell in the store or crack the Hot 100. Culture has deemed that an object with sex appeal creates an aura of allure and creates a buzz of intrigue in the consumer.

We have all heard that sex brings power—we see that in the ads on TV and in the music video that played ten minutes ago—but the fact is this mentality has become such a social condition that sociologists have named this cultural phenomenon *performative sexuality*. "Sociologists have termed this phenomenon Performative Sexuality, noting that often this very public display of sexual power is often completely disconnected from one's personal sex life."[18] When you hear the term, you would think that it's talking about how you perform sexually with your spouse, but that could not be farther from the truth. Performative sexuality

---

[17] Sayers, Mark. *The Vertical Self* (Nashville, TN: Thomas Nelson, 2010), p. 60.

[18] Sayers, Mark. "Beneath the Surface of 'Sexy': The Cautionary Tale of Brigitte Bardot," *Mark Sayers*, May 1, 2009, http://marksayers.wordpress.com/2009/05/01/beneath-the-surface-of-sexy-the-cautionary-tale-of-brigitte-bardot/ (accessed August 28, 2010).

needs to be understood as an often very public display of sexual power that is completely disconnected from a person's sex life. "What is important is not what is going on in someone's real life, but how she, or he is putting on for the audience of their peers..."[19]

Sex is no longer private, passionate, or even special; sex is now a cultural phenomenon lived out in front of our peers for the whole world to see. Two questions need to be addressed for this cultural shift to be understood.

1) How did we get here?
2) How do we become agents of transformation?

The simple answer to the first question is the Internet and the technology boom that has occurred in your lifetime. The arrival of Google, Facebook, and video-sharing sites has changed how the world communicates and has made it easier to create silo lives (we will talk more about this later).

Think about it. When was the last time you said you would email someone? Or do you now tell them you will Facebook them? For myself, email was the shift away from phone calls and letters and was a shift based on time management. I could email ten people in the time it would take to call one person. Facebooking instead of emailing has been a shift based on ease and instantaneity.

How often do you check Facebook each day?

---

[19] Sayers, Mark. *The Vertical Self* (Nashville, TN: Thomas Nelson, 2010), p. 62.

Do you have Facebook on your phone?

Facebook is now a feature on most phones and some phones sold now are social-media-focused. Their sole goal is to make staying connected easier and more convenient in our hurried lives. This has become a change in culture. It has gone from telegrams to letters, phone calls to email, and now to Facebook.

How many of your friends are on Facebook? Or should I ask, how many of your friends are not on Facebook?

Facebook now has over 500 million users.[20] I used to be able to say that Facebook's population made it the fifth largest country in the world, but then something remarkable and unheard of happened. In eleven months, Facebook grew its user market by one hundred million users and has continued to grow at an alarming rate. Nothing in existence has ever grown that much in such a short time. *Time Magazine*, in May of 2010, released an article entitled *How Facebook Is Redefining Privacy*. The article was a study on the privacy issues that have plagued the social media mogul, but it also established how popular Facebook has become.

> Facebook will officially log its 500 millionth active citizen. If the website were granted terra firma, it would be the world's third largest country by population, two-thirds bigger than the U.S. More than 1 in 4 people who browse the Internet not

---

[20] Fletcher, Dan. "How Facebook is Redefining Privacy," *Time Magazine*, May 20, 2010, http://www.time.com/time/business/article/0,8599,1990582,00.html (accessed May 20, 2010).

> only have a Facebook account but have returned to the site within the past 30 days.[21]

Facebook has become such a cultural staple in households throughout Canada that more than half of us are users. Facebook has also become all about sharing. The same *Time* article explains our fascination with what we share.

> Facebook has changed our social DNA, making us more accustomed to openness. But the site is premised on a contradiction: Facebook is rich in intimate opportunities—you can celebrate your niece's first steps there and mourn the death of a close friend—but the company is making money because you are, on some level, broadcasting those moments online. The feelings you experience on Facebook are heartfelt; the data you're providing feeds a bottom line.[22]

Facebook is about making connections between what you share and what others share. It is all about emotionally connecting, but the question needs to be—what are we emotionally connecting to?

> The experience is designed to generate something Facebook calls the Aha! Moment. This is an observable emotional connection, gleaned by videotaping the expressions of test users navigating the site for the first time.[23]

---

[21] Ibid.

[22] Ibid.

[23] Ibid.

The giants behind Facebook have come up with a number of Aha! Moments that a user needs to emotionally connect to in order to join. Which means that Facebook is created to garner emotional connections. They even play on your emotions if you try to leave the site and deactivate your account.

> And if you ever try to leave Facebook, you get what I like to call the Aha! Moment's nasty sibling, the Oh-no! Moment, when Facebook tries to guilt-trip you with pictures of your friends who, the site warns, will 'miss you' if you deactivate your account.[24]

The ease of emotional connection and the play on that connection by those who run the site is what scares me about how easily we share our experiences on the site.

Do we share too much without thinking about the consequences?

Do we have anyone in our lives who can keep us accountable with what we share?

Maybe it is a friend, a sibling, or a family member?

Is your parent a friend on Facebook?

The problem with the Internet explosion is that it will never forget. I just asked if one of your parents was your Facebook friend. I am not telling you that you have to add your parents on Facebook, but I am suggesting that they might be the only filters between what you post and do not post on your page.

---

[24] Ibid.

Do you really want your parents to see those drunken photos from last night?

If you don't care about your parents seeing the photos, then how about your college administrators or future employers?

Most of us would say no, but we post them anyway with the thought of deleting them later. The problem is that Google and the rest of the Internet does not forget. That is what scares me about the photos and content that is posted on Facebook, because many of you miss this point.

What you post tonight will be there for your children to see.

You may be saying, "Brett, that is years away and I don't have to worry about them being able to find pictures of me online." Think about it this way: how much better are you on the computer than your parents? Do your parents come to you for advice with their computers? What I hope you realize is that, like you, the next generation (your kids) will be that much better at surfing the web than you. In the next five, ten, and even fifteen years those half-naked photos you took last night, or those photos of you drunk and passed out in front of a toilet, will not be that funny anymore.

Do you really want to explain that photo to your ten-year-old child someday?

I can look back online and find message boards that I posted on fourteen years ago while I was at university. The message boards are no longer active or even updated today, but thanks to Google what I posted years ago is still there, available to read, never to be forgotten.

Whenever someone adds me on Facebook, the first thing I will do is click "accept," and then I will check out their photos. Usually what I see breaks my heart. What breaks my heart is that the same girls who were just at one of my talks going on about justice, faith, and their relationship with God are in front of me once again. The difference is that what went from a great conversation about living out their faith at school or at home has been tainted because of the photo of her pushing her breasts together in front of a mirror for a photo on her Facebook page. The same eight-year-old girls who talk regularly about truth and justice are taking porn shots of themselves... and everyone thinks it's normal.

What are we doing about the message of self-worth when porn shots on Facebook are the norm?

The guys I meet are no different. I once met a particular boy from a Christian high school. He was, in fact, the student president of the Christian association at his school and he added me on Facebook after one of my talks. So like I said earlier, I went to see his pictures. The first picture on his profile page was him smoking pot from a bong. This is the president of a Christian association and he is sending the message that it is okay to smoke illegal drugs and post the photo along with it.

Do you not see where the message of living out our ancient faith with our modern day culture is lost?

It's not just speakers like me who check out your photos online and question your motives and heart. In an episode of *Dr. Phil*, Dr. Phil had on two girls who were confused as to why they did not get into college. They were confused because they were above average students with GPAs in the high 80s. But for some reason they did not get into university. The recruiters from the university were on the episode as well and very bluntly told the girls that the content they found online kept them from being accepted into the university of their choice.

Here is how the conversation broke down. The recruiters referred to pictures on their Facebook profiles that had them facedown, passed out in front of a toilet. What it looked like was a late night out that took a turn for the worse. The girls denied that the pictures were of them, to which the recruiters pointed out that it was one of their first pictures on Facebook. The point they were making was that the pictures painted a very bad image of the girls' lifestyle choices, which the university did not want to be associated with.

Universities and businesses are now aware of the social networking boom and have started taking advantage of the information that is available. A resume is no longer the piece of paper you send; it's become your top 10 results when they Google search your name. Like no other time in history, a future employer or school administration board can find out the very intimate details of your life. The fact is they will look at what the Internet says about you so that they can protect the integrity of their company or school.

Instead of them protecting their integrity, should we not be more worried about our integrity by what we post online?

Do you know how much it costs to have your history erased on the web? It costs ten thousand dollars to have your past erased, so that Google's claim of never forgetting becomes null and void. The problem is that it is not you who makes the payment. Do you have ten thousand dollars lying under your mattress that you're not planning to use for anything? Or for school? It would be your parents who pay for your past to be erased. If you live like most students out there who hide their Internet self from their parents, you will have even more explaining to do.

Facebook has begun to change and shape the way we live. It allows for ease of communication and has provided an easy way to share our experiences with those closest to us. However, we have to be careful what and who we share our experiences with. Our lives are shaped by how others perceive us, and if we pervert the image we have for ourselves it is easy to become misjudged by others.

The Pornification of Culture

Why has it become so easy to pervert our own lives? How has it become so easy for others to have a perverted view of each and every one of us? If you are over the age of twenty, you have witnessed what I like to call the "Pornification of Culture." Movies, music, and people have all eased up on what they consider too sexy or too racy. David Dark, the author of *The Sacredness of Questioning Everything*, challenges everyone to question how we have arrived at such a perverted state. His book begins at the point where we label others as hot, cool, handsome, and most often sexy.

> Reducing a person in this way is perversion, reducing them in the worst kind of way to an image for visual craving; it is a taking of the human form to market. A not-to-be-objectified beauty is reduced to the easy access of the voyeur whenever a person is primarily good for looking at.[25]

Do we want to be known as only being good to look at? Is that how we want to be remembered? That would quite possibly be the worst tombstone ever written: "Here lies Jon Smith. A father, a son, and a husband, but most importantly he was nice to look at." That would be horrible, but that is the message we hear every day in most of the music we listen to. Take an honest look at the lyrics of some of your favourite songs, or even pick a few off the radio. What do they tell us about each other and the opposite sex? What do the songs tell us to value or strive for?

I will say this: I believe that the pornification of culture is done. Why do I say that, even after I wrote that anyone over the age of twenty has witnessed its arrival? Simple. We witnessed the arrival, the takeover, and now we have reached the lowest point it can possible go. We now let kindergarten kids watch and listen to pornography, which I will dive into deeper later when we talk about the *Transformers* movies.

How many of you have little brothers and sisters who have heard the songs we are about to cover? (See the chart just ahead.) Kids as young as two years old are experiencing

---

[25]Dark, David. *The Sacredness of Questioning Everything* (Grand Rapids, MI: Zondervan, 2009), p. 76.

a pornified culture that has reached its lowest point, because it is considered normal. As you work through the Top Ten songs to follow, I think you will start to agree.

Let's try a little exercise. Here are the Top Ten songs from Billboard.com and the Canadian iTunes Store—at least, at the time this book was written. The next step in our exercise is to figure out what these songs are all about. What worldview do they promote? What values are lifted up? What do they make idols out of? Is anyone objectified or perverted in the lyrics? What does the song say is normal? All these questions will help us paint a picture of the world these songs invite us into.

SONG	ARTIST	WORLDVIEW
California Gurls	Katy Perry, feat. Snoop Dogg	Hot Girls + bikinis = sex on the beach.
OMG	Usher, feat. will.i.am	Lust is the ruling emotion.
Airplanes	B.O.B, feat. Hayley Williams	Fame does not equal happiness.
Billionaire	Travie McCoy, feat. Bruno Mars	Money = happiness.
Find Your Love	Drake	One-sided relationship.
Your Love Is My Drug	Ke$ha	Love is like being high.
Alejandro	Lady Gaga	Sex.

SONG	ARTIST	WORLDVIEW
Cooler Than Me	Mike Posner	What cool is.
Not Afraid	Eminem	Addictions.
Break Your Heart	Taio Cruz, feat. Ludacris	Emotions are cheap, so play with them.

Your turn! Take ten minutes to go look up songs on www.billboard.com, www.mtv.com, or www.muchmusic.com. You can even look through your iTunes store.

SONG	ARTIST	WORLDVIEW

SONG	ARTIST	WORLDVIEW

Now, what do these songs tell you? Ask the same questions I asked about the songs that were on my list. What is normal? You might ask, "Why do I need to go and look up lyrics if you just did it for me?" Simple. This allows both of us to stay current and relevant in our knowledge of the media that is out there. The songs I wrote down were relevant when I wrote this book, but when you read this book those very songs are probably out of date. Music, like movies, are always changing. When we stop paying attention to what is new, we lose touch with reality.

Many of these songs become normal in our everyday lives. We hear them in the car with our families, at school, at work, and at home. When we hear them, we sing along and think nothing of it. Have you ever taken the time to actually listen to the words our little brothers and sisters begin to sing?

One thing I need to note is the connection between the songs on the radio and the music videos we see on Much Music or MTV. For example, let's take Eminem's video for *Not Afraid*. The song has a positive message behind it when it comes to addictions and overcoming your addictions, but it is really hard to pick up on that message when you watch the video. In the song, Eminem talks about why he made the decision to clean himself up and move past his addictions.

> It was my decision to get clean. I did it for me. Admittedly, I probably did it subliminally for you so I could come back a brand new me. You helped see me through and don't even realize what you did. Believe me you, I been through the ringer, but they can do little to the middle finger. I think I got a tear in my eye. I feel like the king of my world. Haters can make like bees with no stingers, and drop dead. No more beef flingers, no more drama from now on. I promise to focus solely on handling my responsibilities as a father, so I solemnly swear to always treat this roof like my daughters and raise it. You couldn't lift a single shingle on it. Cause the way I feel, I'm strong enough to go to the club or the corner pub and lift the whole liquor counter up 'cause I'm raising the bar. I shoot for the moon, but I'm too busy gazing at stars, I feel amazing and…[26]

However, when you see the video for the first time the message can get lost because the video looks like any other Eminem video. The messages may be easy to look at on paper, but the positive messages are easily lost in translation. First, if we watch the video, what does it tell us?

---

[26] Eminem, Kobe, P!nk, Lil Wayne, and Rihanna. *Recovery*. (Santa Monica, CA: Aftermath Records, 2010).

> Images of Eminem breaking through a brick wall further carry the "recovery" theme, symbolizing his battle against alcohol addiction and prescription drugs. Other signs of the rapper's desire for change: a promise to never let his fans down again and "to focus solely on handling my responsibilities as a father."[27]

If you are a Grade Three student watching the video on Much, are you able to understand all the hidden metaphors within the video? Or are you just seeing Eminem acting and sounding like the old Eminem? *Not Afraid* proclaims the rapper's "decision to get clean"—but not without his customary cuss words. Eminem uses six variations of "f—" and three of "s—" in the four-minute song. The song also includes crude uses of the words "crap," "damn," "dick," and "middle finger."[28] Although Eminem's *Not Afraid* music video is chalk full of positive messages, when it comes to drug addiction there are many factors within the song and music video that can blur our lenses when it comes to understanding the worldview the song is portraying. The ability to question and look deep within the words and images of Eminem's video is difficult, especially when you are seeing and hearing them for the first time.

Let's take a quick look at a couple of the other songs on the list. First, let's start with Usher and *OMG*. Hopefully at

---

[27] Afable, Melissa. "Culture and Media Institute," *Culture and Media Institute*, June 8, 2010, http://www.cultureandmediainstitute.org/articles/2010/20100608170031.aspx (accessed June 8, 2010).

[28] Ibid.

this point you all know what OMG stands for, but just in case you don't, it stands for "Oh My God"—not "Oh My Gosh," as the song claims. Who actually says "gosh"? Or more accurately, who means "gosh" when they use OMG in a text?

Anyway, here is a male in his early thirties (born in 1978), singing a song about boobies and booty. "Honey got a booty like pow, pow, pow/honey got some boobies like wow, oh wow."[29] Are you telling me an accomplished artist and creative mind like Usher cannot come up with better lyrics than this? The sad part is we have heard this from Usher before, when he released *Here I Stand...* and it was even done in two parts. "And now we're making love in this club/And we're not gonna stop/Just because the people in the club are watchin' us/Cause we don't give a damn what they say."[30] All three songs are about the same thing—a guy and a girl hooking up and having sex on the dance floor while everybody is watching.

If I asked you what type of music you like, you would probably not answer with, "Songs about sex." The reality is that most of the songs getting radio play are about sex, living large, and being idolatrous.

Ke$ha's songs *Tik Tok* and *Your Love Is My Drug* are all about this worldview. I took my kids to school recently and there was a young girl, maybe in Grade Two, walking along with her ear buds in and singing loudly to Ke$ha's music.

---

[29] Usher, Nicki Minaj, Ludacris, will.i.am, and T.I. *R V R.* (New York: LaFace, 2010).

[30] Usher, Young Jeezy, Will.i.am, Jay-Z, Beyoncé, and Lil Wayne. *Here I Stand.* (New York, NY: LaFace Records, 2008).

Out of the mouth of a Grade Two student comes, "Wake up in the mornin' feelin' like P-Diddy (Hey what's up girl)/Grab ma glasses I'm out the door I'm gonna hit the city (Let's go)/Before I leave brush ma teeth with a bottle of Jack/'Cuz when I leave for the night I ain't comin' back."[31]

Here is a young girl singing about waking up hungover, drinking some Jack, and going back out to party. My question is, does she even know what "Jack" refers to? Probably not, but it is normal because everybody listens and sings to songs without even questioning the influence they have in their lives. I have a concern when a Grade Two student is singing about getting drunk.

Katy Perry has just released what has been marketed as the song of the summer in *California Gurls*, which features Snoop Dogg. It has also been mentioned as a possible anthem for the state of California in the same way that Frank Sinatra's *New York, New York*—or more recently, Jay-Z's *Empire State of Mind*—was an anthem for New York. There is one big difference, however, that sets *California Gurls* apart. It does not look at the greatness of California; instead it focuses on a minority. The song is all about hot girls and their stereotypes.

How would you feel if you were a young girl living in California struggling with your identity and beauty and you hear this song everywhere? Every girl in California who has any value whatsoever must be "unforgettable/Daisy Dukes, bikinis on top/Sun-kissed skin, so hot will melt your Pop-

---

[31] Ke$ha. *Animal*. (United States: RCA/Jive, 2010).

sicle."[32] Apologies to any fair-skinned young women in California, or any girl with modesty who does not stroll around in short shorts all day... according to Katy Perry, your value is diminished. What kind of world do we live in when our girls are starving themselves to look a certain way because the media tells them they have to be a beach babe in order to have any value?

At one point in her life, Katy Perry went by the name Katy Hudson and released a self-titled album under the music label Red Hill. My daughter Zoe still listens to it and even now Katy Perry regularly comments on her religious beliefs and upbringing. In an interview in Blender magazine, first published in October 2008, she spoke about her Jesus tattoo on her wrist. "I see it every time I'm playing guitar. It's looking back up at me. That's where I come from, and probably where I'm going back to."[33]

In the August 19, 2010 issue of *Rolling Stone*, Katy Perry says very public dispute with Lady Gaga over the Alejandro video stems from her religious background.

> "I wrote that tweet because of a combination of things," says Perry. "I am sensitive to Russell taking the Lord's name in vain and to Lady Gaga putting a rosary in her mouth. I think when you put sex and spirituality in the same bottle and shake it up, bad things happen. Yes, I said I

---

[32] Perry, Katy and Snoop Dogg. *Teenage Dream*. (New York: Capitol, 2010).

[33] Perry, Katy. "Culture Clips," *Focus on the Family's Plugged In Online*, October 13, 2008, http://www.pluggedin.com/cultureclips/2008/october132008.aspx (accessed August 10, 2010).

> kissed a girl. But I did not say I kissed a girl while f—ing a crucifix."[34]

Although she is very blunt about what makes her uncomfortable when it comes to sexuality and religion, she is making many Christian girls who love her music feel that exact same way. The tweet she referred to was "Using blasphemy as entertainment is as cheap as a comedian telling a fart joke."[35] If we are going to talk about Katy Perry and the religious journey she is on, it means nothing if we do not take things one step further. There is no sense talking about her coming back to a religion she feels confused about if we are not willing to pray for her and her journey. It is about time that we start praying for the lives of the very artists we are so quick to judge.

I have gone into churches that have been playing Lady Gaga. "Hold me and love me/Just want to touch you for a minute/Baby three seconds is enough for my heart to quit/Let's have some fun/This beat is sick/I wanna take a ride on your disco stick/Don't think too much just thrust that stick/I wanna take a ride on your disco stick."[36] In a world where we are called to flee sexual immorality of any kind, this should not be played during our youth times. It goes against the very worldview we are called to live.

Have you seen the video for the song *Alejandro*? I will save you the time and energy; it is Lady Gaga in her bra and

---

[34] Grigoriadis, Vanessa. "Sex, God and Katy Perry," *Rolling Stone*, August 2010, p. 47.

[35] Ibid.

[36] Lady Gaga, Colby O'Donis, Space Cowboy, and Flo Rida. *The Fame*. (Santa Monica, CA: Interscope Records, 2008).

underwear walking around. At the end, she takes her top off and nine or ten guys fall on top of her.

Yes, sex sells, but it will only take you so far. Lady Gaga is a phenomenal artist, so why does she have to rely on sex to sell albums? There are many artists out there who have commented on how talented she is. T.I. recently told MTV that her talent is shown through her ability to work with a wide range of artists that span numerous genres. "She is a phenomenal talent, and I think that talent transcends through all genres, all races, all religions, all countries,"[37]

He continued in the same interview to point out why she has become so successful through her immense talent. "I believe that that's one thing that everybody can agree on. If you like a song and I like a song, then we going to both dance and all that here together… I think that that's what she's the best example of."[38]

You can even look at the fact that Lady Gaga's talent was showcased on the very successful first season of *Glee*. She has also worked with the likes of Beyonce and Elton John. Her talent is unmistakable, but again it comes down to how the talent is interpreted. Is her talent clouded by her questionable sexual innuendoes and suggestive lyrics, or does it shine through in her musical and vocal talent? The only way to answer those questions is to question the worldviews of the songs and videos that artists put out.

---

[37] Ziegbe, Mawuse, and Kelly Marino. "MTV News," *MTV*, June 28, 2010, http://www.mtv.com/news/articles/1642544/20100628/t_i_.jhtml (accessed August 5, 2010).

[38] Ibid.

Is sex all we are really looking for when it comes to the music we listen to?

I will take the most simplistic sexual line ever. Rihanna is one of the hottest artists on the planet and, in case you don't remember, her boyfriend Chris Brown a couple of years ago abused her. What we need to look at is that 47% of teenagers believe she deserved it.[39] Almost half of your friends, schoolmates, and family think she deserved to be abused by her boyfriend. Both individuals are responsible for the events that occurred that evening. However, we need to understand that violence is a selective response. We can blame all kinds of factors when it comes to our actions, but the actions we carry out and act upon are controllable. We don't punch a cop when we get a ticket, we don't bite a teacher for a failing grade, and we do not scratch at our pastor's flesh when he challenges us on our words and actions.

Guys, I want you to pay attention to this: your size alone can be intimidating enough. I am a big guy and my size alone can be intimidating when I walk into a room. If I wanted to, I could use my size to my advantage, but I don't. Intimidation is just as selective as striking out against someone. Let that sink in a little bit. And ladies, there is no reason, ever, for which you deserve to be hit or abused in any way. Learn that and live by that every day. There is never anything you can say or do to deserve anything.

---

[39] Hoffman, Jan. "Teenage Girls Stand by Their Man," *The New York Times*, March 18, 2009, http://www.nytimes.com/2009/03/19/fashion/19brown.html?_r=2&pa (accessed June 5, 2010).

"Brett, what if she cheated?"

I was actually asked that once. My response is simple: "Then you break up with her. You don't hit her."

The sexual reference in her song goes like this: "I want to see how you move it… You wanna come get me outta my dress?"[40] Is this acceptable? Is this normal? How about for a Grade Four student? How about my daughter? She is in Grade Three. No one would think it is okay for my daughter to sing a line like that, but for us it is okay because we justify that it is just a song and the words are harmless. We live in a world filled with what I call a stratified sexual immorality, meaning that in kindergarten we should listen to none of these songs but then slowly begin introducing them into our lives.

The pornification of culture has penetrated much deeper than the lyrics of our favourite songs. Video games have also been introduced to the notion that sex outsells everything. Gaming today is bigger than music, and perhaps even bigger than television, but I can actually remember a time without video games. That's right—NO VIDEO GAMES!

Then one day there was Pong. That's right, the game with two white rectangles and one circle. That was my video game life, and then everything changed. I could turn that little white ball green and at that moment I told my buddy that I had arrived because I could now change the color of the ball. What else could I want?

---

[40] Rihanna, Jay-Z, and Ne-Yo. *Good Girl Gone Bad*. (New York: Island Def Jam, 2007).

Well, we also had a game called Skeet Shooter. Not too far from Pong in terms of graphics, but there was one big difference—full color. I can still remember a conversation I had with a girl about the relevance of this game and the difference between my generation and her generation.

"Notice how he only had one arm?" I asked.

She said, "You are wrong. That is his gun."

"Well, honey, then he has no arms."

We didn't care about the arms, because we had video games. Would you be so satisfied if all you had was Pong or Skeet Shooter? We didn't even care about change of scenery. Pole Position had mountains that never changed. You could drive in a circle and they would always look exactly the same.

Could you handle that?

Honestly?

I would also play games like Asteroids, Pac Man, Ms. Pac Man, and of course Donkey Kong. Donkey Kong has made a comeback recently, but has been rebranded, as my six-year-old son reminds me every time I say "Donkey Kong."

"DK, Dad! DK!"

Now we can buy all these games together on one console. It's called the Arcade Collection.

Video games have changed dramatically since the days of Pong and Donkey Kong. Video games are now the norm in households instead of the exception. Video games are now online, handheld, and even wireless. Arcades are a thing of the past because everyone has access to some sort of video game every day in North America. Gaming is bigger than TV, bigger than movies, music, and the reality is that what I knew as gaming isn't gaming anymore. It has changed dramatically over the years.

The reality of gaming can be found in the enormous sales of the video game franchise Grand Theft Auto. The franchise has sold almost 90 million copies worldwide, with just about half of those sales coming from North America.[41] The amount of units sold places it well within the top ten video game franchises of all time. I tell you this because unlike some of the other franchises on that list, the reality and worldview promoted by Grand Theft Auto is not biblical. The reality of the game is that I can drive around, pick up a prostitute, have sex with her in the car while she screams out the F-word, and then kill her when I am done.

One night I was scheduled to speak to a youth group and I walked into the building to find the group and the youth pastor playing video games on a big screen. They were playing one of the Grand Theft Auto titles—more specifically, the youth pastor was playing it. When I walked in, the game was on a scene where the characters on-screen were engaged in sexual acts. The youth pastor stopped playing to come over to meet me and asked what I was going to be speaking on that night. I paused in confusion and said, "You."

What is that?!

Is that really what is normal today?

---

[41] VG Chartz, "Software Totals," *VG Chartz*, http://www.vgchartz.com/worldtotals.php?name=Grand%20Theft%20Auto (accessed June 10, 2010).

The reality of culture is that we are now giving games like Grand Theft Auto to kindergarten students because it is a normal game for young kids in lower grades. When you go to Wal-Mart and buy a game that says nudity right on the cover, you need to ask yourself what you're doing.

What is the difference between buying that game and renting porn?

However, it wasn't these online video games that caused the first stir in the pornification of video games. One of the first games was Custer's Revenge, a game in 1982 that had such objectionable content that Atari ultimately sued the game's developer, Mystique, in an effort to publicly distance the Atari console from the game's negative media attention. The game was developed to be a dramatic historical recreation of the battle of Little Big Horn, slightly rewritten to appeal to growing adult fantasies of the time. Instead of being killed by the savage, godless Sioux and Cheyenne Indians, Custer walks through arrow fire to engage a woman tied to a cactus.

MMO (massively multiplayer online) have taken off and provide players with new online lives and experiences. Websites like www.raptr.com allow users to log in and track the amount of hours they spend playing MMOs and their other favourite games through an Internet connection. It also allows you to see how many hours other online users are spending playing these games. If you play these titles, try keeping track of how long you are playing them over a one-week span. Some of the most popular titles are:

MMO TITLE	AVG. HOURS PLAYED (JULY–AUGUST, 2010)
World of Warcraft	4,888,921
FarmVille (Flash)	124,857
Second Life	26,150
Rune Scape	3,828
Guild Wars	83,202
Mafia Wars (Flash)	58,493
Star Craft II	177,541

MMO TITLE	HOURS PLAYED DURING ONE WEEK

The key to understanding the MMO fad is found in the addictive component of these games, especially the MMOs like World of Warcraft, Star Craft, and even FarmVille. Originally World of Warcraft started with sixty levels, but then an expansion came out with another ten, and then they released *another* ten levels. Now this trend is even more evident in the games on Facebook—the problem is that these games do not finish. Every time you get to the end of World of Warcraft, they add a new level to download. IMBU is a chat program, but now you can climb on my lap and give me a virtual lap dance as you chat online with me. The world has changed dramatically. Another attraction to these games is the ability to create and live our lives through siloed lives. This is my silo for school, and this is how I am with my parents.

Do you have two Facebook accounts? One for parents to see, and another you do not tell them about? One where you can lead your clean life with your clean pictures, and another where you can say all the WTFs you want without your parents even knowing?

Texting is another huge problem. To be honest, I love it, but my problem is not with texting. The problem I address today is an emerging trend in culture centering on sex and texting—we call it "sexting." First off, it's an extremely dumb name. It is not just an issue of two people writing sexual messages back and forth, though. The problem I run into is the young woman who takes a half-naked picture of herself and emails it to her boyfriend. The boyfriend is an idiot and then sends it to his friends. A recent study says that one-fifth of all forwarded pictures are sent beyond the initial receiver, which means that any private picture, no matter what the guy says, is usually sent to his friends and beyond. I then get calls asking, "Brett, what do I do? It's all over my school!"

It doesn't matter whether the picture was meant to be private of not. Once it gets shared, the law is the solution. The solution is to charge the girl with creating child pornography. I deal with young Christian girls in Grade Seven who are charged and are now considered registered sex offenders. The boy is charged with distributing child pornography and is now a registered sex offender as well. And so are any of their friends who have the photo on their phone.

Think about that for a second. One mistake and your life is turned upside down because of one simple picture.

Role models today are just awesome—you cannot hear me say this right now, but know that there is a strong sarcastic tone in my voice. Rihanna has been quoted as saying, "If you don't send your boyfriend naked pictures, then I feel bad for him..."[42] *Really?* Her influence is not just with the teens she influences, but preteens as well. It is quite possible that your younger sisters are hearing that they should send naked photos to the boys they have a crush on. Rihanna has actually admitted to feeling humiliated. "I just felt like my whole privacy was taken before that, and then, when that came out, I thought, 'Oh great, so now there's

---

[42] Collins, Leah. "Rehanna's Relationship Advice," *Vancouver Sun*, November 27, 2009, http://www.vancouversun.com/entertainment/Rihanna+relationship+advice+send+your+boyfriend+naked+pictures+then+feel/2276859/story.html (accessed August 2010, 2010).

nothing they don't know about me and my private life.'"[43] Sure doesn't sound like it was a good decision to me.

Is there ever a time when we just say we won't do something? This should be that time. There is no reason why any of us should be sending pictures like that to one another.

How many TV shows do you watch per week? There are so many TV shows today, not to mention all the shows available per season on DVD. Do you watch any of these? What do you watch regularly? How many hours do you watch per night?

TV SHOW	WHAT YOU WATCH	HOURS SPENT
Two and a Half Men		
How I Met Your Mother		
Jersey Shore		
90210		
Desperate Housewives		
True Blood		
One Tree Hill		

[43] Ibid.

What about *Two and a Half Men*?

If you have seen it, I want you to watch it again. You can actually do this next activity with any of the shows you watch… and you might be surprised. Watch the show with a pad of paper and a pencil. I want you to record every time you see or hear something that is sexual in reference. I think you will be surprised at your final outcome. I know I was.

I have actually found between 50 and 75 sexual references in one episode. The show is only 22–24 minutes long! At the end of the episode, I want you to look at the page and ask yourself what kind of shows you actually like. If it is shows like *Two and a Half Men,* then you like shows about sex, because this show is about one thing—sex. Two characters who are trying to get sex and a son who says things he probably shouldn't.

Obviously, *Two and a Half Men* is not the only show like this. *90210* had an oral sex scene in the first ten minutes and *Gossip Girl* has even featured a threesome. The creators and marketers of *Gossip Girl*, when they released their new ads featuring the acronym O.M.F.G., knew they were marketing sex to teens and tweens. Yet in interviews these creators describe their ads as "well-written headlines that are provocative and would catch our viewers' attention… and, in a tongue-in-cheek way, capture what the show is about."[44] The show is about sex and what passions the writers can manipulate the best. These writers are trying to teach that these are normal teenage lives, but normal lives

---

[44] People, "OMG! Check out the sexy new Gossip Girl Ads," *TV Watch*, July 23, 2008, http://tvwatch.people.com/2008/07/23/omg-check-out-the-new-gossip-girl-ads/ (accessed July 3, 2010).

should not look anything like this. Take that same chart we filled out above and do the same thing, but this time instead of filling in the hours spent watching TV, fill in the number of sexual references you hear or see.

TV SHOW	SEXUAL REFERENCES	SHOW LENGTH
Two and a Half Men	50–75	22–24 minutes
How I Met Your Mother		
Jersey Shore		
90210		
Desperate Housewives		
True Blood		
One Tree Hill		

How are shows all about sex working for you?

How do shows about sex relate your ancient faith to your modern world?

Movies are no different.

I could list hundreds and hundreds of movies that have come out in the past, in the present, or are soon to be released that focus on sex. Would you watch a movie that is full of the following topics and values?

> Sexual slang, including many crude anatomical references, abounds. Sex-related dialogue also includes topics ranging from pubic hair on teenage boys to elderly women using sex toys. Anal and oral sex, orgasms, masturbation, pornography, tampons, losing one's virginity, genital size and "loud, intense make-up sex" also garner verbal attention.[45]

The fact is, you probably did—the film was *I Love You, Man*. After one talk, a kid came up to me and asked if I was talking about the Unrated or Restricted version. I said it did not really matter, nor did I particularly care what version the film was.

The boy, he was in Grade Seven.

He said he had seen both and didn't know which one I was talking about.

I really didn't know where to go with a kid that young.

"Ruder, cruder, and nuder"—How do you connect your faith with that?

When a film is labeled unrated, do we really understand what it is saying? Some parents think, "Oh, it hasn't been rated yet." What it really means is that they pulled stuff out of it to get it a restricted rating. They will actual pull item-by-item, scene-by-scene, and object-by-object until they get the right rating. Then they throw it all back in and place it in Blockbuster.

---

[45] Keffer, Lindy. "Video Reviews: *I Love You, Man," Focus on the Family's Plugged In Online*, http://www.pluggedin.com/videos/2009/q2/iloveyouman.aspx (accessed August 10, 2010).

The new way that movies are being butchered is through something called a "Producer's Cut." In my time, it was Oliver Stone redoing *Pearl Harbor* in a different way. He would edit and change the ending. Now they take a woman, naked, and walk her back and forth in front of a blue screen. They then add her to the movie.

That isn't a "producer's cut." That is nudity for the sake of nudity.

I actually had someone ask me what *Zack and Miri Make a Porno* was about. It is about Zack and Miri making a porno! Do you really need to ask me what it is about? It is a new love story, right? They fall in love after they have sex in a movie. Director Kevin Smith, when faced with a NC-17 rating, argued his way down to a simple R rating.

> Look, if I were a 13-year-old boy, and I saw [*Zack and Miri Make a Porno*] on cable back in 1983? Yes, it would [make me masturbate]. Now, as a 13-year-old boy, if I saw this movie? It would not titillate me. I would simply go to the Internet and watch real people having real sex. How can you possibly say this is too erotically charged when it's so obviously a comedy with people having over-the-top fake sex, when we can see examples of real sex at a keystroke?[46]

Kevin Smith used today's acceptance of porn as a logical defense for his film's final rating.

---

[46] Smith, Kevin. "Culture Clips ," *Focus on the Families Plugged In Online*, October 13, 2008, http://www.pluggedin.com/cultureclips/2008/october132008.aspx (accessed August 10, 2010).

For the first time ever this year, we had a date rape scene in a movie which we now call funny. *Observe and Report*, with Seth Rogen. He's on a bed having sex with a passed-out woman, who has puked… that's called date rape. I deal with date rape about a hundred times a year. I deal with the suicide, cutting, hurt, and pain that comes along with that. The woman wakes up and says, "Did I not tell you to stop, mother f—er?" And we call it funny. The actress even said in an interview that she didn't know where that was going to go.

> So when we were shooting it, even the date-rape scene—or as I refer to it, "The Tender Love-Making Scene"—I just thought, "We'll shoot it, but it's not gonna be in the movie. I don't have to worry about that one." And yet there it is… I've got this all wrong. I don't understand the tone of this movie at all. I think it's really difficult for an actor to get a sense of that when you aren't a part of the project from the beginning.[47]

Movies have changed when even the actors begin to question the reasoning behind the script, the tone, and even the grand scheme of the films they are in.

What is the most disturbing movie you have ever seen?

I have asked over 200,000 people this question in about three years and three people have agreed with me and said that the most disturbing movie they have seen is *Transform-*

---

[47] Tobias, Scott. "Interview Anna Farris," *A.V. Club*, April 7, 2009, http://www.avclub.com/articles/anna-faris,26245/ (accessed July 5, 2010).

ers. Transformers was a concept originally made for my generation. Growing up, I would leave basketball practice, run home, and watch *Transformers*. When I tell people that, I usually get inhales. People cannot believe that the most disturbing movie for me is *Transformers*. I say, watch it again with a piece of paper and write down all the sexual innuendos. I had one question when I saw the first *Transformers* film: why was a five-year-old beside me on opening night in a booster seat?

In my mind, I actually looked at the dad and said, "You're an idiot." Honestly, he's five. It is a PG-13 movie; it says so right on the trailer. An organization that knows nothing about Christ says you should probably be thirteen to watch this. It has sexuality and violence written right on it. As I am thinking these lovely yet inappropriate thoughts, the whole row in front of me fills with Grade One students and the row behind me fills up with Grade Two kids. How do I know that the pornification of culture, mentioned earlier, is done? It is done when we are giving the discussion of masturbation to kindergarten kids. My kids are six and seven and hardly understand sexuality, let alone talking about what masturbation is. The same can be said about the discussion in the film about the porn magazine called Busty Beauties.

Megan Fox is being used in these films as a form of eye candy. She does not act or say anything of relevance, and yet she is okay with that. In an interview with *Entertainment Weekly*, she was asked about her experience of being a "club girl" in the movie *Bad Boys*, what it was like and how she felt about being used. "I thought it was awesome. I was going to a Christian high school and I wasn't a feminist yet. I hadn't sat back and analyzed society yet. I was 15! I just did what I was told to do."[48] It is like *Baywatch* redone. She just runs for half the film. She hardly has any lines and does basically nothing. In the second film, she is drawing and you can't even see what she is doing. The goal was to see up the back of her jeans.

What is interesting about Megan Fox is that she feels this should be every girl's dream. In the same interview, when asked about purely being a sex symbol actress, she says it is empowering.

> It doesn't bother me. I don't know why someone would complain about that. That just means that the bar has been set pretty low. People don't expect me to do anything that's worth watching. So I can only be an overachiever. I think all women in Hollywood are known as sex symbols. That's what our purpose is in this business. You're merchandised, you're a product. You're sold and it's based on sex. But that's okay. I think women should be empowered by that, not degraded.[49]

The message she gives in *Transformers* is the same message she gives in reality. Set your bar low and rely on beauty to get you what you need.

---

[48] Nashawaty, Chris. "Megan Fox: 'Fallen' Angel," *Entertainment Weekly*, June 10, 2009, http://www.ew.com/ew/article/0,,20284375,00.html (accessed April 15, 2010).
[49] Ibid.

I was recently asked by someone why his kids were swearing so much. I explained as easily as I could, "Well, my kids watch films like *Bolt* and *Madagascar*. Your kids are watching *Scary Movie 4*, and they are in kindergarten and Grade Two. Your son has watched *Watchmen* and you bought *Transformers* for your kindergarten son." My kids might hear "Bum" from time to time, and they think fart is a bad word. Go figure! One day, my daughter Zoe came home from school and informed me that she now knew the F-word. I hesitated for a moment and then asked her what she had learned.

"Fart," she sheepishly told me. To her, that is a bad word because in her context, based on her age and the media in her life, that's as bad as it gets. Why do we need to expose children to excessive violence and sexuality before they can even understand what it is all about? Does a kindergarten student understand what a porn magazine is, or masturbation for that matter? So why are we allowing them to watch movies that speak so openly about those topics?

Is the new normal to expose ourselves to topics before we understand what they are all about?

I will not let my son watch *Transformers*, and it is hard because I do not think there is a single friend of his who has not seen it.

It is time that we begin to ask ourselves what values we are picking up from the films we watch.

When *Transformers 2* was released, I pulled into the parking lot of the theatre and prayed, "God, please don't give me content for my talks at the movie. I don't care for more content." I just hoped that the crazy parenting experience of the first film would not repeat itself and that I could just watch. I sat down with my drink and popcorn and took a look around. To my astonishment, there was only one other man and woman. That was it. There was just one problem, though. I couldn't figure out why the theatre was so loud. Then I saw the twenty-three four-year-olds between the man and woman. It was a birthday party and I literally sat with tears in my eyes and filled nine pages of notes on my iPhone. Here is a sample of what the audience was exposed to during *Transformers 2*:

- "Kiss this, b★★★★!"
- "I'm gonna skinny dip and you can say s★★★ about it."
- "It's an a★★ kicking!"
- "Park my foot in you're a★★!"
- "That's my eye, you crazy b★★★★!"
- "Had sex with her in my dream."
- "Pop a cap in his a★★."
- "He's an a★★hole!"
- "Oh s★★★!"
- "I am directly below the enemy scrotum."

I have three issues with *Transformers*.

- You and I think it is normal. We just go see movies and we do not question what we are taking in. Everything becomes normal.

- Parents have stopped parenting. How many movies do you have in your collection that have a rating higher than your age? How many of those movies have been given to you as a present for whatever reason? Instead of stirring the pot, parents give in and buy movies because of pressure.
- The writers. Michael Bay does not write this film alone. He sits down with a team of writers. My question is, who sits down as a team and decides to put testicles on a robot? I don't remember that in the original cartoon. How about the line, "I'm directly below the enemy scrotum"? Who thought that should go in? Is it necessary? How does it pass through a team of writers, multiple viewings, and still end up in the final cut of the film? If those are some of the best ideas you can come up with, then you are a pathetic writer and should switch jobs.

There are a million things to talk about in films like *Transformers*, because no one walks out of a movie and says, "I just loved the discussion on masturbation." Those types of discussions are irrelevant, yet many of the films we watch are just laced with this type of material. I have friends who have recently seen films like *Sex and the City 2* and *Kick Ass* and sat through them with tweens and their parents.

Kick Ass came out this year to very mixed reviews. Comic fans loved and hated it and critics did not know how to take Chloë Grace Moretz and her Hit Girl alter ego. One of her main lines in the film is, "I never play." This would not be so bad if she wasn't at an age where she should be enjoying the innocence of preteen life. However, these are very fitting words from Hit Girl in the movie and I found them to be some of the most chilling. As an eleven-year-old actor and character in the film, the actions of Hit Girl are disturbing, to say the least. She is the main killer in the movie and has no regard for human life whatsoever. The message that comes through her actions is a desensitized one. Killing isn't a game in this movie; it's second nature. There is one scene shot from the same angle and viewpoint of a single person shooter, sort of like the one that *007: Golden Eye* (for Nintendo 64) made famous. We are also shown a filmed execution that gets played over the Internet. In an age when we witness this on the news, do we really need to see it in a movie? Does this give the message that nothing shocks us as a culture anymore?

Has media, especially movies, become the one indulgence we allow in our lives? Do we look past everything that contradicts our biblical worldview?

How about *Iron Man* and the stripper pole on the plane, or the multitude of scantily clad "cheerleaders" during the opening of *Iron Man 2*? The latest *Crank* film had only one sequence that was not filled with blood, gore, skin, sex, or profanity—and it only lasted about ninety seconds.

The Bible is quite clear, yet we do not talk about Mark 9:42 often: *"On the other hand, if you give one of these simple, childlike believers a hard time, bullying or taking advantage of their simple trust, you'll soon wish you hadn't. You'd be better off dropped in the middle of the lake with a millstone around your neck.*" This is a direct warning about causing young people to sin. I think many writers, directors, producers, and actors in Hollywood, Vancouver, and Toronto need to take these words to heart. The actions and values played out in their films are influential to all of us, yet many times they go unquestioned. We also need to take these words to heart and realize we are being manipulated into thinking this is normal; once we think it is normal, we fall away from the ancient faith we are trying to follow.

Sexuality is a huge conversation and Ephesians 5:3–4 is a great place to start. *"Don't allow love to turn into lust, setting off a downhill slide into sexual promiscuity, filthy practices, or bullying greed. Though some tongues just love the taste of gossip, those who follow Jesus have better uses for language than that. Don't talk dirty or silly. That kind of talk doesn't fit our style. Thanksgiving is our dialect."* There's more to sex than mere skin on skin. Sex is as much a spiritual mystery as a physical act. As written in Scripture, the two become one. *"We must not pursue the kind of sex that avoids commitment and intimacy, leaving us more lonely than ever—the kind of sex that can never 'become one'"* (1 Corinthians 6:16–18).

A student said to me recently, "Can my girlfriend give me oral sex or not?"

The fact is this: we want a yes or no answer, and that's it. Not some line about how it's not about what we *can* do sexually, like it says in Ephesians, because that is too confusing for us to interpret. The question should not be how close you can get to your guy/girlfriend, but how close you can get to God in your relationships.

Let's take a look at the downward slide. It starts with holding hands, which leads to kissing, which eventually leads to oral sex and intercourse. First, I want to say that holding hands is fine and I say that because I have to. I have to because I deal with suicide attempts all the time involving people who have said that if you touch a girl before you are married you are sinning before God.

A guy once came up to me weeping—not just crying—and says this in between weeps: "Girlfriend… beach… parents… sex…"

Okay, so he got caught by his parents on the beach having sex. It seemed easy enough to decipher. This interpretation, however, wasn't even close.

He was on a beach in northern Ontario walking with his girlfriend. Her parents were behind them holding hands. Then his girlfriend reaches down… and at this point I pause, but it's okay. She grabs his hand.

"Okay," was my response.

"Brett, I read a book that said if you touch a girl before you marry you are sinning before the God you love." As the conversation continued, he said, "I had my first suicide attempt that week." The day I got to him was his second suicide attempt and he was ready to try for the third time.

There are times when I just don't know what to say. I said, "When my daughter is in Grade Seven or Eight and she is walking on the beach holding hands and I am behind her, I pray for that every day of my life." His shoulders shrunk right down and he started to cry. The guilt placed upon kids is amazing. Holding hands is nice, but everything else is a problem.

The Bible is very clear when it says to flee from sexual immorality. It is the only place in the Bible I can think of where it says to more than merely not do something; it actually says to *flee and run* from sexual immorality.

Sexual immorality is defined as being sexually fulfilled in any way, shape, or form with anybody other than your spouse, whether you are married or not. It includes sex, oral sex, and masturbation.

I have had students ask me, "What about foreplay?" Be careful of this slippery slope, because even before you begin going down it, you give away your heart. We give away our hearts very quickly to people we really do not even know. Oftentimes we give it to people who will only be close to us for a short period of time. Sexual immorality covers much in the middle portion of that slope and the whole middle section is foreplay. Foreplay is designed to get you excited for sex.

Dr. Louann Brizendine explains why it is so easy to fall down the slope.

> If testosterone were beer, a 9-year-old boy would be getting the equivalent of a cup a day. But a 15-year-old would be getting the equivalent of two gallons a day. This fuels their sexual engines and makes it impossible for them to stop thinking about female body parts and sex.[50]

---

[50] Brizendine, Dr. Louann. "Love, sex and the male brain," *CNN Opinion*, March 25, 2010, http://www.cnn.com/2010/OPINION/03/23/brizendine.male.brain/index.html?hpt=C2 (accessed August 10, 2010).

These developing hormones are uncharted territory for most young males. That is why understanding the differences between desire, lust, and biblical love is essential. Without knowledge, one cannot help but fall down the slippery slope of desire.

What makes you different from the millions of other people who cannot stop themselves from sliding down that slippery slope? In my fourteen years of speaking, almost all the students who hit the bottom of the slide say they regret it.

If we really want to avoid saying "I wish I didn't," we need to come up with some practical things to help us not go down this slide.

I tell guys all the time, "Don't lie on a couch with your girlfriend lying down in front of you."

For a guy, having his girlfriend lying down in front of him will turn him on incredibly. So just don't do it. Don't lie down anywhere. Just sit up. If you are going to struggle with being alone, then don't surround yourselves with things that will help you slide down that slippery slope.

"Don't excite love, don't stir it up, until the time is ripe—and you're ready" (Song of Solomon 8:4).

When are you ready? When you have given your heart for the last time. When you find the person who will be with you forever and not just for a season. For most of you, you are not at this point. If you say, "I don't care what God says," and then choose another god to worship, you are offering up your body as a living sacrifice to your boyfriend or girlfriend instead of to God. At that point, it becomes a problem of worship.

In all my research on dating, it seems that all relationships you are in up until Grade Eleven don't make it. If we could bet right now with students who are in Grades 7–11 on whether or not their relationships will work, no one in their right mind would make that bet. You may be thinking that your parents met in high school and it worked for them, but that was then and this is now and chances are it will not work for you. You would never give up your money on a bet that is going to lose 100% of the time, so why are high school students all over the continent willing to give up their sexual purity before giving up their money?

There are at least three possible outcomes when it comes to sexual immorality and they are: HIV, pregnancy, and STD/STIs. One in four teenage girls now has an STD, and that number is growing. Girls, there is a message you need to hear—sex affects you more than it does your boyfriend. It will always affect you more than a man. There is a greater chance of you getting an STD, and the big gamble is pregnancy. Being a single teenage mother in Canada is the single largest factor in determining whether or not you will live below the poverty line for the rest of your life. I am not trying to use fear tactics when I say that, but that is the reality. Scaring anyone into abstinence and celibacy is not the way to make this reality known, but knowing the possible and realistic outcomes of sex before marriage is the only way to know how important a decision it truly is.

I work and speak to thousands of people and I hear a lot of "I wish I had waited," or "I didn't know." But living with a guilty conscious for the rest of your life is not God's way either. We live and serve a forgiving God who is full of grace that redeems us in his eyes. Praying and asking for forgiveness with an earnest heart leads us into the redemptive arms of God. Do some people break out and escape the hardship of single parenting? Sure. But most don't! For that stat to change drastically, it is up to men to step up and take part in raising the kids they leave behind. It also begins with making a similar vow to the one Job makes: *"I made a solemn pact with myself never to undress a girl with my eyes"* (Job 31:1).

Have you seen the commercial for Miller Genuine Draft entitled "Nothing to Hide"? In this commercial, a guy has a girl over to his house for a date and she is searching through his DVD collection, only to come across *Bikini Babes on Mars*. She asks him about the movie only to hear the response, "It's a classic." The reason it's on the shelf with all the other DVDs is that they are all arranged in alphabetical order. She shrugs it off and continues to look through the collection as if to say that is normal.

All students go through media awareness now, and they are all taught that commercials lie—not just some commercials, all commercials. The question becomes what is that lie? If I don't have that car, I won't have the girl. If I don't wear that brand of clothing, I won't look good. I'm too ugly, too fat, too poor. Whatever the commercial is saying, it is a lie. The sad thing about this commercial is that she is saying it's okay (a porn video, alphabetized and out in the open). It's normal, she says. On how many levels is this wrong?

This commercial is telling the lie that:

1) It makes sense to have porn.
2) It makes sense to keep your porn out in the open, etc.

It is about time we make the same kind of decision Job does. Porn is not okay; it is a serious problem that is everywhere in our culture. Once again, where is your line? What do you view as okay or acceptable when it comes to porn? We use porn in everyday language, even inside the church world. One of the big sayings on Facebook is "porno boobs." There are tons of photos out there and all we comment on are boobs.

Also, what have you called sexy today? The fact is that many of the photos put up on Facebook look like they have come right out of a porn photo shoot. Have you noticed how stripper poles have appeared in many different media sources? You can buy exercise programs centered around pole dancing. They are on Brooke Hogan's TV show regularly, as well as in Paris Hilton's photo shoots. Is that where your line is? Is it okay to exercise in a porn atmosphere while watching a porno is completely out of the question?

A 2008 survey by www.xxxchurch.com stated that the average age anyone is introduced to Internet pornography is eleven. That same eleven-year-old child cannot get into a theatre on their own to see *Twilight*, *Robin Hood*, or *Iron Man 2*, yet many of them have had, or can gain access to, Internet porn. There are approximately 420 million pornographic webpages online, making up over 12% of the total amount of websites available. Worldwide porn revenue exceeds 96 billion dollars, which is more money than the revenues of every major league sport combined.

The normalization line, which measures the acceptance of pornography in mainstream culture, is also on the rise. Porn is everywhere and it is up to us to make a decision about how we handle it.

> Our culture is becoming increasingly sexualized and it has taken forty years to go from one dirty magazine under the counter at the local convenience store to today where it is expected that junior high boys have at least one nude shot of their junior high girlfriend on their cell phone.[51]

Where have you drawn your line?

Porn has crossed many lines in popular culture and has become more and more visible on daytime TV. Jenna Jameson was on Oprah on November 19, 2009. Why is this a big deal, you may be asking? When the biggest porn star in the world is on Oprah, times have changed. Porn used to be found in brown paper bags or on the top shelf of the convenience store. But now the biggest porn star ever is featured on one of the most popular shows ever. That is why it is such a big deal.

Porn has become a normal and acceptable part of our culture and worldview. On the program, Jameson kept saying no regrets, no regrets, and no regrets. She said, "I don't

---

[51] Driscoll, Mark. *Porn-Again Christian: A Frank Discussion on Pornography & Masturbation* (USA: Mars Hill Church, 2009).

know what I am going to tell my kids." She cried as she said this, but the thing is, you can't say there are no regrets and then wonder what you are going to tell your kids. God tells us how to escape this type of regret. *"So here's what I want you to do, God helping you: Take your everyday, ordinary life—your sleeping, eating, going-to-work, and walking-around life—and place it before God as an offering"* (Romans 12:1).

Where does lusting fit into this type of life?

It doesn't!

God many times speaks out against whoring our bodies, as he calls it.

> At the head of every street you built your lofty place and made your beauty an abomination, offering yourself to any passerby and multiplying your whoring. You also played the whore with the Egyptians, your lustful neighbors, multiplying your whoring, to provoke me to anger. Behold, therefore, I stretched out my hand against you and diminished your allotted portion and delivered you to the greed of your enemies, the daughters of the Philistines, who were ashamed of your lewd behaviour. (Ezekiel 16:25–27, ESV)

How about the words in Ezekiel 23:18–21?

> When she carried on her whoring so openly and flaunted her nakedness, I turned in disgust from her, as I had turned in disgust from her sister. Yet she increased her whoring, remembering the days of her youth, when she played the whore in the land of Egypt and lusted after her paramours

> there, whose members were like those of donkeys, and whose issue was like that of horses. Thus you longed for the lewdness of your youth, when the Egyptians handled your bosom and pressed your young breasts. (ESV)

The fact is, God spoke boldly about sexual immorality and was aware that it was a big problem. If God can address the issue, why can't we? Lust has become such a huge influence in culture for teens and young adults that it has begun to affect their future.

> About one-third of college men today describe difficulty achieving and maintaining erections, which is a stunning figure. Thirty years ago it would have been way less, more like 5%. I think the major reason is that if a boy's primary sexual activity has been masturbating to pornography, he's going to find it harder to achieve an erection with an actual girl who's not wearing lingerie, who's talking…[52]

Just like God speaking to Israel in Ezekiel, we need to be honest with ourselves about the severity of unholy desires in our lives.

How can we fix the problem?

Accountability software. I run Covenant Eyes (www.covenanteyes.com) and X3WATCH (www.x3-

---

[52] Fillion, Kate. "How to fix boys," *Macleans Magazine*, January 9, 2008, http://www.macleans.ca/culture/entertainment/article.jsp?content=20080109_70985_70985 (accessed August 10, 2010).

watch.com). I can go home tonight and go onto any porn site I want, but tomorrow I will have two guys calling me, asking, "What's up?" There is nothing more frightening than having your personal life under a microscope by those closest to you, but that accountability, if you're honest about moving past an addiction, is the only way to succeed.

Self-Injury

There is no issue in our world today that brings up more emotional feelings than the issue of self-harm. Henri Nouwen, one of my favourite authors, says, "Our life is full of brokenness... How can we live with that brokenness without becoming bitter and resentful except by returning again and again to God's faithful presence in our lives?"[53] I am a Christian and a follower of the way. Do I believe God can heal? Yes, I do.

Do you?

Do I believe God is there, in our healing? Yes.

Again, do you?

I will, however, part ways with the faith questions for a moment, because this is what I hear all the time: "Brett, I talked to my pastor, I talked to my youth leader, I talked to my whoever, and I told them I am struggling with cutting and their response was to pray to Jesus and you will be fine." Then they leave the room.

---

[53] Nouwen, Henri. *Sabbatical Journey: The Diary of His Final Year* (New York, NY: Crossroad Publishers, 1998), p. 134.

I will acknowledge that God can heal, but let me say this: that answer, to me, is religious abuse. We are called to be the hands and feet of God.

> The way God designed our bodies is a model for understanding our lives together as a church: every part dependent on every other part, the parts we mention and the parts we don't, the parts we see and the parts we don't. If one part hurts, every other part is involved in the hurt, and in the healing. If one part flourishes, every other part enters into the exuberance. (1 Corinthians 12:24–26)

If you or someone you know is hurting because they cut or harm one another, and you have heard this, I am sorry. All of us are called to be people who stand beside each other, care for each other, and help heal one another. But we don't. We walk away, over and over again.

So yes, I acknowledge my faith, but how do we be the hands and feet of God?

Personally, I explain self-injury as hurting yourself in any way, shape, or form, with anything you could ever imagine, to get beyond overwhelming feelings and emotions.

A man actually yelled out at one of my talks, outright yelled from the crowd, "Why would you ever talk about this?"

I flipped my slide and he quietly sat back down in his seat.

In 2008, *The Globe and Mail* published results from a Canadian study finding that one in six teens are injuring themselves through the act of self-harming.[54] Most of us who speak on, or in the field of, helping kids who self-harm would place it more in the range of one in five. The man who yelled at me saw these same stats. This is a growing issue that needs to be addressed because people who are unfamiliar with self-harm and why it is happening have a very skewed opinion on the subject.

One of the first things I hear when I talk about this subject with teens is, "Yeah, I know that kid. They're emo." If you think the only person who struggles with self-harm wears black more than someone else, you are just wrong. There is no "that" person, there is no nationality, there is no ethnicity and age… it does not matter, because anyone can struggle with self-injury. The youngest person I have dealt with is in Grade Three and the oldest is a seventy-seven-year-old. Self-injury does not pick and choose based on anything.

Last year, at an event called Creation, I was speaking on the main stage and announced that I would be speaking during a breakout session later that day on self-injury and if anyone wanted to know more, they could come by. At least three people said to me after my main stage talk that no one would show up for a breakout on self-injury. It is funny how things work out. Those three people were all in the front few rows when I spoke to the four to five thousand

---

[54] Picard, André. "One in six teens inflict self-harm." *Globe and Mail,* January 29, 2010, http://www.theglobeandmail.com/life/article663414.ece (accessed on July 10, 2010).

people who showed up that afternoon. We were in a forest and we could not move. After the talk, I stayed to talk with those who were there and a couple walked up. They said that they had been about to leave when the husband turned to his wife.

"Honey, I cut," he said.

She went on to tell me that she ripped into him, thinking he was joking and kidding around after my talk. But then she noticed the tears.

"Brett, I thought people who cut were Goth, wore black all the time, or they were people who wear long sleeve shirts in the summer. Brett, I am a fifty-year-old youth pastor. I wear Abercrombie and Fitch. Cutting isn't exclusive, because that is who I am."

Cutting affects so much more than a gender, ethnicity, or cultural subgroup. The reality is that even as you are reading this book there will be people who acknowledge for the very first time that they self-injure. They will admit to themselves that they no longer want to live that way and no longer want to live in silence. How can I be so sure of that, you ask? The answer is quite simple. There are a lot of people hurting in silence and many who struggle with self-harm every day. When I am away speaking, there are usually a few people in the crowd who will come up and acknowledge the fact that they are cutting, or hurting themselves in other ways.

There is no particular look for someone who struggles with cutting. Notice that I did not say a "cutter"—I hate labels. If you deal with cutting and you are reading this book, note that you are not a "cutter." It is your struggle.

You can and will get beyond it. It is not your identity. It is not who you are. It is not the only thing you are about.

I once read the following statement: "You are infinitely more rich than any single label might say."

Self-injury can include eating disorders like anorexia, bulimia, and binge eating. Self-injury can include cutting. This is the conversation for today. Self-injury is suicide and this is a conversation I have with people on an ongoing basis.

I get calls like this from the very schools you attend. Someone from the school might say, "Brett, we just had a Grade Four kid hang himself. Can you come and speak to the students?"

First off, what kind of world are we living in when we have Grade Four students who do not want to be a part of it any longer? My response is always the same: "No, I can't."

I am not a crisis team and this book won't have all the answers, because I am not a counsellor. In reality, there is no speaker in the world who can walk in and make things okay… because things are not okay. If you are reading this book and are thinking about suicide, or you struggle with self-injury, please contact a counsellor, or visit www.yourstory.info.

When I talk about drugs and alcohol, I am not talking about addiction. We are talking about people who do these things to get beyond something in their lives. We are talking about that bad day that happens from time to time, and let's be honest—six beers work. I am not saying it's okay to go and drink six beers if you have a bad day; I am saying that when drugs and alcohol are used in that way, it is an escape from something we see no end to.

We know there is hope on the outside. People say they live in this dark hole in their head and they just don't know how to get out. Maybe you feel like Job when he is talking to God about his life. Here is a guy who could really go for those six beers to escape his broken spirit.

> My spirit is broken,
> my days used up,
> my grave dug and waiting.
> See how these mockers close in on me?
> How long do I have to put up with their insolence?
>
> O God, pledge your support for me.
> Give it to me in writing, with your signature.
> You're the only one who can do it!
> These people are so useless!
> You know firsthand how stupid they can be.
> You wouldn't let them have the last word, would you?
> Those who betray their own friends
> leave a legacy of abuse to their children.
>
> God, you've made me the talk of the town—
> people spit in my face;
> I can hardly see from crying so much;
> I'm nothing but skin and bones.
> Decent people can't believe what they're seeing;
> the good-hearted wake up and insist I've given up on God.

But principled people hold tight, keep a firm
grip on life,
sure that their clean, pure hands will get stronger
and stronger!

Maybe you'd all like to start over,
to try it again, the bunch of you.
So far I haven't come across one scrap
of wisdom in anything you've said.
My life's about over. All my plans are smashed,
all my hopes are snuffed out—
My hope that night would turn into day,
my hope that dawn was about to break.
If all I have to look forward to is a home in the
graveyard,
if my only hope for comfort is a well-built coffin,
If a family reunion means going six feet under,
and the only family that shows up is worms,
Do you call that hope?
Who on earth could find any hope in that?
No. If hope and I are to be buried together,
I suppose you'll all come to the double funeral!
(Job 17)

God goes on to tell Job that he is the hope Job needs. This is quite a funny conversation between God and Job because God presents Job with a situation that is impossible to accomplish on his own. God asks Job, *"Or can you pull in the sea beast, Leviathan, with a fly rod and stuff him in your creel?"* (Job 41:1) Basically, can you go out on a boat and catch the Lock Ness Monster with a fishing pole? God again asks Job, *"What hope would you have with such a creature? Why, one look at him would do you in!"* (Job 41:9)

Is this not how we feel when we look into the black hole we think we are living in? Do we really think we can get past our own situations? God is essentially saying, "If you can't hold your own against my glowering visage, how then do you expect to stand up to me? Who can confront me and get away with it? I'm in charge of all this—I run this universe!" Do we take our bad days and turn them into a Leviathan? Do we think the only way to get beyond our struggles is drugs and alcohol? If so, the question becomes, where are you putting your hope?

Is it in God or in drugs?

The Bible speaks about hope over and over again. 1 Thessalonians 5:6–11 encourages us to place our hope in each other, our faith, and in God.

> So let's not sleepwalk through life like those others. Let's keep our eyes open and be smart. People sleep at night and get drunk at night. But not us! Since we're creatures of Day, let's act like it. Walk out into the daylight sober, dressed up in faith, love, and the hope of salvation. God didn't set us up for an angry rejection but for salvation by our Master, Jesus Christ. He died for us, a death that triggered life. Whether we're awake with the living or asleep with the dead, we're alive with him! So speak encouraging words to one another. Build up hope so you'll all be together in this, no one left out, no one left behind. I know you're already doing this; just keep on doing it.

I want you to read a poem that was posted on my Your Story page (www.yourstory.info). This poem addresses the very question we have been looking at above—where are you putting your hope?

> Only His Blood can heal our wounds. How did it come to this, how did my eyes not see? How can I be waking up with scars and bruises instead of joy and life? When did the dark begin to override the light, and will the light come back? I believed you. You told me and I believed you. And now I am here, bruised and scarred, with only the words resonating in my mind (only His blood can heal our wounds, only His blood can heal our wounds). Oh please, take it back, take me back, make me beautiful. Make my scars a memory that doesn't burn, and make these bruises the verdict of what was, not what is. I believed you. You told me and I believed you. I want to be whole again. I want to breathe again. I want to live again. I want to wake up tomorrow and these bruises be gone, and these scars never come back. I am better than this (only His blood can heal our wounds, only His blood can heal our wounds). You promised me beauty for ashes, beauty for ashes. Take these ashes and make them beautiful. They are burnt and bloody and dry, but I know you can make them beautiful. These ashes are the sin that ate at me, convinced me, lied to me, told me these bruises I deserved. I believed you. You told me and I believed you. Make the ashes beautiful (only His blood can heal our wounds, only His blood can heal our wounds). This is the final show. This is the last day I wake

> up like this. Today I will wear my bruises and scars as a sign, that tomorrow the light will come back… and His blood will heal my wounds…[55]

Where is your hope? Is it in things that can drag us back down, or is it in the blood that can wash us clean?

There are two types of people who are reading this book, and even more accurately there are two types of people in the world—

- Those who self-injure, and
- Those who know someone who self-injures.

When I speak at your schools and ask the group if they know anyone who struggles with eating disorders, cutting, drugs, etc., the whole room puts up their hands. We all know someone who struggles, but how do we respond to that person? Is it with religious abuse, or with a message of hope?

How many people do you know who struggle with self-injury in any form?

In her book *Cut,* Patricia McCormick says this, "There are all kinds of things in the world you could use to hurt yourself. All kinds of things you could turn into weapons. Even if you wanted to give them all to me, it would be impossible… I can't keep you safe, only you can."[56] If you are reading this today and you are that person, realize that you

---

[55] Annonymous, "His Blood," *Your Story*, http://www.yourstory.info/content/view/132/12/ (accessed August 5, 2010).

[56] McCormick, Patricia. *Cut* (Asherville, NC: Front Street, 2000), p. 126.

are the only person who can stop. No pastor, no teacher, no person can tell you to stop; it has to be you, when you come to a place where you can say, "This doesn't work." Out of five thousand emails I have received from those who self-injure, not one of them ever says it is an easy way to cope. Instead, all they say is that it's the only way they know how to cope.

Is that you?

Is self-injury the only way you know how to cope with a bad day, bad relationship, bad grades, or anything else that has gone wrong recently? It has to be you. Karen Conterio, in her book *Bodily Harm*, says this: "There is nobody on earth who can, or will, save you from yourself. You are going to have to do it for yourself—but not by yourself."[57] That means family or friends are not the ones to make you stop. But like in the passage from 1 Thessalonians, they can give you the support you need. Stopping has to be a conscious decision of your own. It won't be easy, but it comes down to where you see hope coming from and who can speak hope into your life. The problem is that we struggle with speaking hope and encouragement into the lives of our friends who are dealing with self-injury.

I hear this all the time: "Brett, I was at this party and a girl pulled up her sleeve and she hurts herself."

"What did you do?" I ask.

"I got uncomfortable and went home."

---

[57] Conterio, Karen, Wendy Lader, and Jennifer Kingson Bloom. *Bodily Harm: The Breakthrough Treatment Program for Self-Injurers* (New York, NY: Hyperion, 1998), p. x.

I will give you the same line my professor gave me during my studies in the Arrow Leadership[58] program: "Suck it up, princess." That is my response. Instead of walking away from someone in need, suck up your pride, suck up your ego, and grow up. I say that to everyone, whether you are four, forty-four, or a hundred and four. It does not matter what age you are. We all need to grow up and look in the mirror in search of the caring human being God calls us to be in Matthew 22.

How can we love our neighbour if we are not willing to stick it out with them through the tough times? If someone in need approaches us and our response is to go away, what message does that send to the person looking for help? Is this promoting our ancient faith worldview? Was that Jesus' response to those who came to him in need? Was that the attitude Jesus took to the cross? Stand your ground, especially if you are a Christian. Explain that you might not understand what they are going through, or even understand their need to harm themselves, but that you will be there for them. We need to start letting people know that we will work through it with them. We need to be willing to go see counsellors with them if that is what they want, or to be available as accountability partners. We need to be there for them as they say, "I am lost and don't know what to do."

Most people who come out of a life of self-injury usually note one person, one person who never left their side. Marv Penner, in his book *Hope and Healing for Kids Who*

---

[58] www.arrowleadership.org

Cut, challenges us to be available to be that one person in the life of a young person who entrusts his or her story to you.[59] We can be that person. We just need to be in the same room as them. I challenge you to start having real conversations with the people you go to school with. Stop having the whole "How are you… fine… good" conversations and start seriously having "No, how are you really?" conversations. That's the only way to start promoting healing and hope to those around us.

Actions are the things we do. Our actions can be forms of self-injury, and I would include promiscuous sex as self-injury. Erwin McManus, the pastor of Mosaic, a church in Los Angeles, says, "Fake intimacy is better than wide open loneliness." I know a lot of teens and young adults who just fall into bed with someone thinking they will find some great closeness or compassion, but all they find is pain, guilt, and more sorrow. But our actions arise from our feelings. The single largest feeling in your generation is the feeling of abandonment, not love, not compassion, not joy— but abandonment.

What do you feel abandoned from?

Our feelings come from something deep, though, and they are our stories, our histories, and we all have them. Some of them are easy to deal with, right? We didn't make the basketball team or we got fired or we failed the test… we can deal with those stories. There are some things, though, that we are just not able to handle.

---

[59] Penner, Marv. *Hope and Healing for Kids Who Cut: The Diary of His Final Year* (Grand Rapids, MI: Zondervan, 2008), p. 26.

A nine-year-old girl once said to me, "Brett, I think I know why I cut and am bulimic."

"Why?"

"Well, my mom left my dad."

"I'm sorry."

"I came home the next day and found my dad hanging in our garage."

Another girl told me this about why she struggles with every form of self-injury I have named: "I go to Western University and I was raped on my first date."

So, what do I mean by dealing with stories? Last year, I had to deal with some things. I had three important people I love pass away in less than a year. My Uncle Bob died of a heart attack, my Aunt Gail lost her life to breast cancer, and the one that rocked me was the death of one of my best friends, Warren Parker. Each death was painful to deal with on their own, but when you add in the pain and feelings of losing multiple people, it became almost unbearable.

Warren's death was a surprise because of the nature in which it happened. A drunk driver killed him. I was the best man at his wedding and it was one of those moments when you just start to fall apart. After each loss, I started to have this feeling of incredible sadness and unbelievable anger weaved together to form this weird new feeling. All I wanted to do was get beyond it. Honestly, six beers would have helped anyone get beyond it, but for how long? Maybe an hour, one hour of freedom, but then an hour later you're back in the same place with the same anger, the same sadness, never dealing with the issue.

How do we deal?

We deal by sitting down with a counsellor. It was fascinating to me that wherever I went after Warren's death, everyone I met on every flight I went on seemed to be a counsellor. This went on for a couple of months. I would have these conversations over and over.

"What do you do?"

"I am a counsellor."

"Really?"

I mean, come on, this was like the fifth counsellor I sat beside. I began to have conversations with people I didn't even know who helped me walk through this conversation. The steps looked something like this:

ACTIONS

FEELINGS

YOUR STORY

First, deal with your root issue. So many of us have deep hurts at our core that we have never addressed. We need to deal with them before we can move forward. Secondly, we need to learn how to deal with our feelings. I know that when I have a bad day, I watch TV. It helps me relax and I can lose myself for a couple of moments in my favourite shows. What I do is different from what my wife does, which is different from what you will need to do. We all do different things to deal with our feelings. Learn what works best for you. Try writing down ten actions that help you deal with your feelings. Maybe it is reading, writing, or drawing. It could be watching TV, listening to the soothing voice of Frank Sinatra… it could be just about anything.

EXAMPLE: WATCH TV
1.
2.
3.
4.
5.
6.
7.

8.
9.
10.

Kill Zones: Violence in Media

The first video game in the first-person shooter craze was not *007: Golden Eye* for the Nintendo 64 game console. It was actually *Maze Wars*, and it was released in 1985. It involved a ball that looked like an eye walking through a maze. It did not even have a gun. Then they made *Phantom Slayer*, and they said they had made the first-person shooter scary. Really, it's just a clear head that moves around. It all started to change after that, but first we had *Duke Nukem*. Essentially it was just Mario with a blond haircut. I don't care what they say, he was a Mario clone.

Doom, to me, is when everything changed. Now we could kill without a gun because we had a chainsaw that could cut off people's faces. In the two years after it was first released in 1993, it is estimated that ten million people downloaded the game. Every single first-person shooter after that is considered a clone of what *Doom* started.

Mike Gummelt from Raven Software said, "We'd have to really be either extremely stubborn, in deep denial, or lying to say that the violence in our games doesn't affect people."[60] In the same breath, he also mentions that games like *Doom* are only the beginning of the problem. "But I don't think it's *Doom* that's the problem, it's the free proliferation and general acceptance of violence in our society. In movies, on TV and (to a lesser degree due to limits of realism) in games. That kind of widespread violence and cruelty in media definitely takes the shock out of violence and gore."[61] *The New York Times* describes the games as "games in which players stalk their opponents through dungeon-like environments and try to kill them with high-powered weapons."[62] It is about time we begin to ask ourselves what games like *Doom* are teaching us. What are they saying is normal, and what do they promote as normal?

We have to begin to ask ourselves, why do we need to live out scenarios where killing is considered a right response, or the way to gain more points? The Bible says, *"You shall not murder"* (Exodus 20:13, NIV). Technically speaking, stepping on a mushroom in Mario Bros. is considered killing, but I think we can all agree there is a huge difference between stepping on a mushroom and decapitating a body for the thrill of it.

However, in Matthew 5:21–22 we are told that hate and anger are just as bad as murder: *"You have heard that it was said to the people long ago, 'Do not murder, and anyone who*

---

[60] Brown, Janelle. "Doom, Quake and mass murder," *Salon*, April 23, 1999, http://www.salon.com/technology/feature/1999/04/23/gamers (accessed August 4, 2010).

[61] Ibid.

[62] Johnson, Dirk and James Brooke. "Portrait of Outcasts Seeking to Stand Out From Other Groups," *The New York Times*, April 22, 1999, http://www.nytimes.com/library/national/042299colo-school-suspects.html (accessed August 4, 2010).

murders will be subject to judgment.' But I tell you that anyone who is angry with his brother will be subject to judgment" (NIV).

Aggressive and excessively violent video games such as *Manhunt* and *Red Dead Redemption* promote worldviews centered on hatred and violence—whereas Mario stepping on a mushroom is not rooted in malice. There needs to be an understanding between what we know is right and what we know is wrong. We know that running through streets, or the Wild West, killing individuals is wrong.

Rockstar Games' newest release *Red Dead Redemption* comes with an M rating—for mature audiences only. It warns the buyer that this game is filled with blood, intense violence, nudity, strong language, strong sexual content, and drug use.[63] The main objective of the game is quite simple and summed up on their official website as: "Red Dead Redemption is an epic battle for survival in a beautiful open world as John Marston struggles to bury his blood-stained past, one man at a time."[64] The video game also condones tying up women and placing them on railroad tracks to gain points and also regularly refers to women as b—s and w—s. Rockstar Games has once again pushed the limits on their graphic video games, taking their controversial worldviews from the streets of Vice City to the wide open plains of the 1960s' western frontier.

In 2000, *Soldier of Fortune* was first created with the aid of an ex-army colonel. The game featured twenty-six kill

---

[63] Rockstar Games, "Info," *Red Dead Redemption*, http://www.rockstargames.com/reddeadredemption/info (accessed August 7, 2010).

[64] Ibid.

zones on the human body and each victim responded differently depending on which "kill zone" was affected, what weapon was used, and how far away the attacker was. All that information was written into the coding for the game. The creators of *Mortal Kombat* were featured in the Summer 2010 issue of *Electronic Gaming Monthly*, which was entitled *Remaking a Legend*. "Mortal Kombat is known for and associated with violence, and we're definitely going back to that." Ed Boon, who is the creative director, tells us everything we need to know about the video game franchise. This game is all about violence. The developers of this game are actually writing into the code how the body would react if an arm was ripped off. This is so that while you are playing you are driven to the final frontier of video game violence, as the article points out.

Do you really need to know how the body would react if an arm was ripped off, or your body cut in half?

Quentin Tarantino has this problem all the time. He asks himself, *What color do I make the blood?* Apparently it's a big deal. "I'm really particular about the blood, so we're using a mixture depending on the scenes. I say, 'I don't want horror movie blood, alright? I want Samurai blood.' You can't pour this raspberry pancake syrup on a sword and have it look good. You have to have this special kind of blood that you only see in samurai movies."[65] Have we become so desensitized to blood and violence that we write

[65] Jakes, Susan. "Blood Sport," *Time Magazine*, September 9, 2002, http://www.time.com/time/magazine/article/0,9171,349193,00.html (accessed April 4, 2010).

off movies because the color of blood was not realistic enough? Quentin seems to think so, as he reshoots entire scenes if the color is off or the sound is not realistic enough.

I don't even think we realize how our minds react to this kind of violence anymore. I do not believe the results of every study that comes out linking violence and behaviour, because for every person who says violence influences you, you can find one who says it does not. However, somewhere there must be a little voice that says this cannot be good; it just cannot be good to expose ourselves constantly to something God tells us to avoid.

I cannot talk about violence in culture without talking once again about Grand Theft Auto. Do you remember the girl we talked about earlier from the game? That's right, the girl you can have sex with well after that you kill her and get your money back. This scene is written into the game. It is the game. Someone sat down and coded that result out. When we golf club a woman in the face in the game, someone during development golf-clubbed a dummy and recorded how it would look. The cheekbone breaks, blood comes out of her face (which was chosen from a color pallet), and she crumbles to the ground. When we kick her on the ground, someone actually kicked something like a sack of potatoes and recorded what it looks like. It sounds foolish, but that girl becomes just as valuable as the sack of potatoes on the ground. When she is dead, you get paid. Welcome to Grand Theft Auto.

I really believe that you cannot tell me you oppose violence against women and play this game, or any other game like it. I stand by that and no one has ever given me a suitable argument against that statement. If you do not believe it, write me an email. My contact information is at the back of the book. Start your email with this line:

"Brett, I believe I can club a women in the face because..."

Have you ever been bullied?

Did you like it?

How did it make you feel?

Would you like to relive the experience in a video game?

Another game I would like to talk about is called Bully. As someone who speaks to numerous victims of bullying, I have to ask if this game is necessary. I deal with kids who are taking their own lives because someone told them their shoes are from Wal-Mart. So what is our answer to this growing dilemma? We bring out a game where we bully people for fun and entertainment. I don't know how that is fun. Bullying becomes justified to thousands of kids who play this game, because now it is fun. This becomes a normal part of their daily routine.

Where are we going as individuals when the games keep getting darker and more violent?

Do you have a limit with violence and video games?

What are your favourite games? What do they say about you?

I am not saying that all games are wrong. I grew up with the video game with the red-and-blue guns where you had to shoot the robbers—and not the innocent people—during a bank robbery. I suppose that was killing, in a sense. Then there are games where you blow each other's heads off and blood covers the screen. Somewhere between the innocence of cops and robbers and the brutality of today's video games there needs to be a balance.

Movies have always been violent. The whole argument that they are getting more violent is not exactly true. Some of the original violent movies are the most violent, like *Reservoir Dogs, Clockwork Orange*, and *Seven. Psycho*, by Alfred Hitchcock, is another, but it didn't really portray violence. You never see the knife go into Janet Leigh's character. You never see it, it was perceived. *The Shining*, which I now call a comedy by today's standards, was quite violent when it was made in 1980.

MOVIE	RELEASE DATE	RATING
Alien	May 25, 1979	Rated R for sci-fi violence/gore and language.
A Clockwork Orange	February 2, 1972	Rated R for strong sexual content and violence throughout including rape, graphic nudity, and drug use. All involving teenagers.
Friday the 13th	May 9, 1980	Rated R for graphic bloody violence, sexuality, and some drug use.
Halloween	October 25, 1978	Rated R for strong violence and terror, language, some sexuality/nudity, and drug use.
Nightmare on Elm Street	November 16, 1984	Rated R for horror violence, language, and some disturbing images.

MOVIE	RELEASE DATE	RATING
Psycho	August 25, 1960	Rated R for violence.
Reservoir Dogs	October 23, 1992	Rated R for strong violence and language.
Seven	September 22, 1995	Rated R for strong graphic violence, some nudity, and pervasive language.
The Texas Chainsaw Massacre	October 1, 1974	Rated R for intense sequences of terror and violent content.
Texas Chainsaw Massacre 2	August 22, 1986	Unrated.
The Shining	May 23, 1980	Rated R.

*All movie info from www.imdb.com.

As we move forward, you have movies like *American History X*, *Gladiator*, *Fight Club*, and the highest grossing R-rated movie so far—*The Passion of the Christ*. That's right. Mel Gibson's portrayal of Jesus' sacrifice is the highest grossing restricted film of all time. Every time we see a new violent movie, we see something new and different. Those "ah moments" take away the disturbed feeling the next time you see it. For myself, one of those moments was when the guy gets shot in the car in *Pulp Fiction*. The movie *Wanted*, staring Angelina Jolie, was called a ballet of brutality as it was violence played out in poetic beauty that changed the way action sequences will be shot forever. *The Departed* also provided some of those as well. The point, though, is from that moment on we are okay with what happened in the film. The next time we see it on film, we will not think twice; it will just be another scene in some movie we watched at some point in our lives.

MOVIE	RELEASE DATE	RATING
American History X	October 30, 1998	Rated R for graphic and brutal violence including rape, pervasive language, strong sexuality, and nudity.
American Psycho	April 14, 2000	Rated R for strong violence, sexuality, drug use, and language.
Fight Club	October 15, 1999	Rated R for disturbing and graphic depictions of violent anti-social behaviour, sexuality, and language.
Gladiator	May 5, 2000	Rated R for intense, graphic combat.
Hannibal	February 9, 2001	Rated R for strong gruesome violence, some nudity, and language.
Kill Bill, Volume 1	October 10, 2003	Rated R for strong bloody violence, language, and some sexual content.
Kill Bill, Volume 2	April 16, 2004	Rated R for violence, language, and brief drug use.
Natural Born Killers	August 26, 1994	Rated R for extreme violence and graphic carnage, shocking images, strong language, and sexuality
The Passion of the Christ	February 25, 2004	Rated R for sequences of graphic violence.

MOVIE	RELEASE DATE	RATING
Pulp Fiction	October 14, 1994	Rated R for strong and graphic violence, drug use, pervasive strong language, and some sexuality.
Red Dragon	October 4, 2002	Rated R for violence, grisly images, language, some nudity, and sexuality.
Saving Private Ryan	July 24, 1998	Rated R for intense prolonged realistically graphic sequences of war violence and for language.
The Departed	October 6, 2006	Rated R for strong and brutal violence, pervasive language, strong sexual content, and drug material.
The Silence of the Lambs	February 14, 1991	Rated R for strong bloody violence, disturbing images, language, and some sexual content.

Everything changed with *Hostel.* After the torturous scenes displayed in *Hostel,* producers began to question whether or not those types of scenes would produce a new genre of film. With the introduction of intense torture in *Hostel*, the door was opened for producers and directors to expose their audiences to new forms of grotesque violence. This birthed a whole new genre of film called "torture porn." You can add all the *Saw* films, *The Hills Have Eyes*, *The Mist*, and *Turistas* to this category. Reactions to *Hostel* were just as intense as the scenes in the movie.

> At the very first screening of "Hostel" at the 2005 Toronto Film Festival, two separate ambulances were called from people having such extreme reactions to the film. One man left the theater during Josh's torture, fainted, and tumbled down the escalator, and during Paxton's torture a woman had festival volunteers call an ambulance, claiming the film was giving her a heart attack. Both patrons were okay, and local media thought it was a publicity stunt by director Eli Roth. Ironically, Roth knew nothing of the incident, as he was in the theater watching the film, and only found out after when he was told by the festival staff of the chaos that transpired.[66]

We have to start questioning ourselves on the movies we watch when they start to invoke such strong reactions when we see them. Yes, it was only two people out of a whole theatre, but does that not make you wonder if we really need to expose ourselves to such graphic and unnatural scenarios?

MOVIE	RELEASE DATE	RATING
Hostel	January 6, 2006	Rated R for brutal scenes of torture and violence, strong sexual content, language, and drug use.

[66] Internet Movie Database, "Trivia for Hostel," http://www.imdb.com/title/tt0450278/trivia?tr0781144 (accessed August 8, 2010).

MOVIE	RELEASE DATE	RATING
Planet Terror	June 21, 2007	Rated R for strong and graphic bloody violence throughout, sexual content, nudity, drug material, and pervasive language.
Halloween Unrated	August 31, 2007	Rated R for strong and brutal bloody violence and terror throughout, sexual content, graphic nudity, and language.
300	March 9, 2007	Rated R for graphic battle sequences throughout, some sexuality, and nudity.
Hostel, Part 2	June 8, 2007	Rated R for sadistic scenes of torture and bloody violence, terror, nudity, sexual content, language, and some drug content.
Pan's Labyrinth	January 19, 2007	Rated R for graphic violence and some language.
The Devil's Rejected	July 22, 2005	Rated R for sadistic violence, strong sexual content, language, and drug use.
Pineapple Express	August 8, 2008	Rated R for pervasive language, drug use, sexual references, and violence.
Resident Evil: Extinction	September 21, 2007	Rated R for strong horror violence throughout and some nudity.
Rambo	January 25, 2008	Rated R for strong and graphic bloody violence, sexual assaults, grisly images, and language.

MOVIE	RELEASE DATE	RATING
Saw 1–5	October 29, 2004–October 28, 2008	Rated R for strong and grisly violence and language. (*Saw 1* was edited for re-rating; it was originally NC-17).
Shoot 'Em Up	September 7, 2007	Rated R for pervasive and strong bloody violence, sexuality, and some language.
The Hills Have Eyes	March 10, 2006	Rated R for strong and gruesome violence and terror throughout, and language.
The Hills Have Eyes 2	March 23, 2007	Rated R for prolonged sequences of strong and gruesome horror violence and gore, rape, and language.
The Mist	November 21, 2007	Rated R for violence, terror and gore, and language.
Turistas	December 1, 2006	Rated R for strong and graphic violence and disturbing content, sexuality, nudity, drug use, and language.
Untraceable	January 25, 2008	Rated R for grisly violence and torture, and some language.
Wanted	June 27, 2008	Rated R for strong bloody violence throughout, pervasive language, and some sexuality.

MOVIE	RELEASE DATE	RATING
Kick Ass	April 16, 2010	Rated R for strong and brutal violence throughout, pervasive language, sexual content, nudity, and drug use—some involving children.

When I have to explain something, I have to ask if I am missing the mark. The point to all this is whether or not we are questioning what we are watching. Are we aware of what these movies portray as being acceptable? Are we aware that the movies we watch change how we view the world?

Let me be brutally honest about violence for a moment. You did not hear me say that if you play GTA (Grand Theft Auto), you will shoot up your school. I cannot tell you how many times people have come to my talks and have heard things I did not say. I do not want that to happen with this book. There are tens of millions of copies of GTA sold around the world and you cannot give me five hundred school shootings in the same time period.

We as Christians need to respond to the world with a smart yet rash commentary. Instead, too often the commentaries we give are reactionary and instantaneous. We see GTA or *Saw* as violent, and then make the conclusion that all violence stems from the increase in violent media. Countless times, a newspaper reports a school shooting and then trot out a Christian who says it is because of Grand Theft Auto. I didn't say that if you watch *Saw* or *Dexter,* you are going to go out and beat someone up. I do not think that is true.

I have been researching this for two years and do not think the root issue in violence is the media itself; the root is found in men. Men are responsible for 98.2% percent of the rapes in the world. Almost all domestic abusers are men. Men lead most violent statistics in the world. Men are the leaders responsible for almost every negative thing that happens on the planet. If we are going to have a real talk about violence, we need to turn away from media and start looking at the men of the world. Most men believe that domination and power over women, and everybody else, is normal. Look at GTA: the lead character is a male. Look at Manhunt, Bully, Gears of War, Soldier of Fortune, or almost any other violent video game or movie out there—the aggressor is usually a male. Do women commit violent acts? Of course, but I believe the root is male.

Jackson Katz is one of America's leading anti-sexist male activists, and on his website he points out ten ways that males can help stop gender violence. His first step reinforces the male role in gender violence. "Approach gender violence as a MEN'S issue involving men of all ages and socioeconomic, racial and ethnic backgrounds. View men not only as perpetrators or possible offenders, but as empowered bystanders who can confront abusive peers."[67] I hope we can all realize that male bashing is not my intent, nor is it

[67] Katz,Jackson. "Ten Things Men Can Do to Prevent Gender Violence ," *Jackson Katz*, 1999, http://www.jacksonkatz.com/wmcd.html (accessed August 10, 2010).

the solution to this issue. It goes back to what we discussed earlier about abuse being selective and controllable.

If we just stopped here, if I just said "Good luck, glad you read this book," I would be wasting your time. The next question becomes, "Now what?"

FAITH

faith

As we look beyond the culture that has influenced our lives, we should ask ourselves, "Now what?"

Where do we go?

What do we do with this information?

How do we move forward?

These questions need to be reflective responses to the cultural influences that surround us every day. If movies, music, and video games are how we see the world working around us, how do we change that? When God's original calling on our lives has been lost in lyrics, ballads, and scripts, how do we get back to that calling? The question—"Now what?"—then becomes a personal journey back to our creator. The only way we can get back to our creator is by acting out our beliefs.

Kary Oberbrunner, in *Called: Becoming Who You Were Born to Be*, explains how beliefs can be integrated into our lives. In Hebrew philosophy, a belief is not a belief until it is acted on. All beliefs affect community because the actions they spawn affect every area of life.[68] This is a challenge for many of us as we go about putting our beliefs into actions. When we move away from this challenge, or fail to engage, we fall into the very dangerous trap of misleading others and ourselves into who Jesus is and what he has called us to do. "I think we have bought into a new Jesus who allows us to live our lives any way we desire."[69]

Paul warns us about this trap in his letter to the Colossians: *"See to it that no one takes you captive through hollow and deceptive philosophy, which depends on human tradition and the basic principles of this world rather than on Christ"* (Colossians 2:8, NIV).

So, what now?

See the Plan

The first step is to let God's original calling and plan be revealed to us. How do we allow God's story to be revealed to us? Simply put, this is the Bible. It is God's word given to us as an instruction manual, the way to life, life in him. The Bible is meant to be our story—our story given to us by a loving God who is constantly at work in the world. "The Bible tells a story. A story that isn't over. A story that is still being told. A story that we have a part to play in."[70]

---

[68] Oberbrunner, Kary. *Called: Becoming Who You Were Born to Be* (Winona Lake, IN: BMH Books, 2007), p. 54.

[69] Ibid., p. 9.

[70] Bell, Rob *Velvet Elvis: Repainting the Christian Faith* (Grand Rapids, MI: Zondervan, 2005), p. 66.

We have been given an opportunity to be a part of God's story, but we need to understand why.

John Taylor, in *A Story-Shaped Faith*, explains how we are to best understand our roles.

> Do you want to understand yourself? Do you want to know the meaning of life, or what you are meant to do? Let me tell you a story: "In the beginning God..." That is the opening line of the story of God's relationship with his creation. In the story, we have both rights and responsibilities. One of those responsibilities is to remember what God has done and tell it to the next generation.[71]

What does God's word say about this idea of storytelling?

> God's Message to Joel son of Pethuel:
> Attention, elder statesmen! Listen closely,
> everyone, whoever and wherever you are!
> Have you ever heard of anything like this?
> Has anything like this ever happened before—
>   ever?
> Make sure you tell your children,
> and your children tell their children,
> and their children their children.
> Don't let this message die out. (Joel 1:1–3)

---

[71] Taylor, Daniel. "A Story-Shaped Faith," in *The Power of Words and The Wonder of God*, ed. John Piper: Justin Taylor, 105-121 (Wheaton, IL: Crossway Books, 2009), p. 113.

Write this down for the next generation so people not yet born will praise God. (Psalms 102:18)

And then he told the People of Israel, "In the days to come, when your children ask their fathers, 'What are these stones doing here?' tell your children this: 'Israel crossed over this Jordan on dry ground.' Yes, God, your God, dried up the Jordan's waters for you until you had crossed, just as God, your God, did at the Red Sea, which had dried up before us until we had crossed." (Joshua 4:21–23)

Place these words on your hearts. Get them deep inside you. Tie them on your hands and foreheads as a reminder. Teach them to your children. Talk about them wherever you are, sitting at home or walking in the street; talk about them from the time you get up in the morning until you fall into bed at night. (Deuteronomy 11:18–20)

And do this so that their children, who don't yet know all this, will also listen and learn to live in holy awe before God, your God, for as long as you live on the land that you are crossing over the Jordan to possess. (Deuteronomy 31:13)

Take to heart all these words to which I give witness today and urgently command your children to put them into practice, every single word of this Revelation. (Deuteronomy 32:46)

This way, your children won't be able to say to our children in the future, "You have no part in God." We said to ourselves, "If anyone speaks disparagingly to us or to our children in the future, we'll say: Look at this model of God's Altar which our ancestors made. It's not for Whole-Burnt-Offerings, not for sacrifices. It's a witness connecting us with you." (Joshua 22:27–28)

Then commanded our parents
to teach it to their children
So the next generation would know,
and all the generations to come—
Know the truth and tell the stories
so their children can trust in God,
Never forget the works of God
but keep his commands to the letter.
(Psalms 78:5–8)

"As for me," God says, "this is my covenant with them: My Spirit that I've placed upon you and the words that I've given you to speak, they're not going to leave your mouths nor the mouths of your children nor the mouths of your grandchildren. You will keep repeating these words and won't ever stop." God's orders. (Isaiah 59:21).

The people of Ephraim will be famous,
their lives brimming with joy.
Their children will get in on it, too—
oh, let them feel blessed by God!
I'll whistle and they'll all come running.
I've set them free—oh, how they'll flourish!

> Even though I scattered them to the far corners
> of earth,
> they'll remember me in the faraway places.
> They'll keep the story alive in their children,
> And they will come back. (Zechariah 10:7–10)

> The promise is targeted to you and your children, but also to all who are far away—whomever, in fact, our Master God invites. (Acts 2:39)

Throughout Scripture, we are given a clear example that God's ways will in fact be passed down through stories, but how do we learn of his stories? It is simple—through the discipline of study. Study has always seemed like such a negative word when it comes to listening and learning the words of God. This is because it holds so many negative memories for us—the late nights studying for an exam, that test we studied all night for and failed anyway, those beautiful June afternoons lost to a world of textbooks.

However, when we study the word of God, the connections with the world around us are nothing like the dreadful days of June exams. Read aloud these words from Rob Bell and listen to the transformation that can come from reading and studying God's word. The world that God's word invites us into is very much the world we are trying to escape from. That is the beauty behind God's story. As we try to escape from our lives, searching for answers, he invites us into his story, which ironically is happening all around us.

> We have to embrace the Bible as the wild, uncensored, passionate account it is of people experiencing the living God. Doubting the one true God. Wrestling with, arguing with, getting angry with, reconciling with, loving, worshiping, thanking, following the one who gives us everything. Real people, in real places, in real times, writing and telling stories about their experiences and their growing understanding of who God is and who they are.[72]

Are these not the questions we are seeking answers to?
Who am I?
Where am I?
What am I doing here?

Experience

When we study God's word on a personal level, we begin to experience, to be able to apprehend the objects, people, events, thoughts, and emotions that we read on the pages. Our senses, thoughts, and experiences begin to take shape before us and we get to personally participate in God's story. This type of learning, or experiencing, is the best way for us to transform our actions based on the beliefs we hold. "The only kind of learning which significantly influences behavior is self discovered, or self appropriated learning—

---

[72] Bell, Rob. *Velvet Elvis: Repainting the Christian Faith* (Grand Rapids, MI: Zondervan, 2005), p. 63.

this is truth assimilated in experience."[73] God meets us on the page in a personal way as we begin to understand our own experiences and God's truths begin to show themselves in our daily lives.

Tony Jones explains discipline and the benefits of studying God's word. "Christians engage in these spiritual practices not out of duty or obligation but because there is a promise attached: God will personally meet us in the midst of these disciplines."[74] This is where our theology forms. We begin to understand the character and nature of our God as we study his words and personally and emotionally experience what he continues to do. The Bible teaches us who he is, what he is like, and what he intended us for. In the end, we begin to see that all stories point to our restoration through Jesus. As stories shape our imagination, we begin to see how big God truly is. Theology allows us to place the story within the meta-narrative.

There are a couple of big words in that last sentence that we should break down together.

Theology, in this sense, is not a deep and scientific word but a simple understanding of who God is through his nature and characteristics. We gain this understanding through what we talked about earlier—studying the word of God. Tony Jones explains how this type of theological outlook can benefit our understanding of God.

---

[73] Miller, Mark. *Experiential Storytelling: (Re)discovering Narrative to Communicate God's Message* (El Cajon, CA: Zondervan, 2003), p.17.
[74] Jones, Tony. *The Sacred Way: Spiritual Practices for Everyday Life* (Grand Rapids, MI: Zondervan, 2005), p. 18.

> And anytime human beings talk of God, they're necessarily also going to talk about their experience of God... In other words, it's how we talk about the points of intersection between God and us, the places where God's activity meets our activity.[75]

How else would we get to know someone better? We learn about God the same way we learn about our friends. By talking with him, listening to his words, and understanding what he likes.

Meta-narrative is the next big word that we need to unpack in order to more fully understand how God works in the world. A meta-narrative is "a grand, overarching, all-encompassing story that gives meaning and order to life—past, present, and future."[76] When we begin to read about him with an intention to gain a better understanding of who he is, we begin to look more like him every day.

> I'm telling you to love your enemies. Let them bring out the best in you, not the worst. When someone gives you a hard time, respond with the energies of prayer, for then you are working out of your true selves, your God-created selves. (Matthew 5:44–45)

God asks us to make a transformation away from our true selves so that we can reflect him, and in doing so the

---

[75] Jones Tony, *The New Christians: Dispatches From the Emergent Frontier* (San Francisco, CA: Jossey-Bass, 2008), p. 105.

[76] Novelli, Michael. *Shaped By The Story: Helping Students Encounter God in a New Way* (Grand Rapids , MI: Zondervan, 2008), p. 27.

scriptures start to become our story as well. When we read scriptures that talk about Jesus, or Jesus teaches us about himself, we need to also ask ourselves questions so that we can better understand him.

What does the story say about Jesus? What is, or who is, Jesus concerned with in the story? What does Jesus value in the story?

Who is Jesus?

Take the time to read the following passages and ask yourself the same questions.

> MATTHEW 25:40, MATTHEW 5:44–45, MATTHEW 9:13, MATTHEW 18:10–14, JOHN 8:12, LUKE 10:25–37, ACTS 20:35, MATTHEW 8:22, MATTHEW 25:41–45, LUKE 4:18–19, MATTHEW 22:37–40, MATTHEW 11:28–30, MATTHEW 25:31–40, MARK 10:17:22, JOHN 10:10–14, AND MATTHEW 16:25–28.

What did those passages say about who God is?

What does he value?

God values compassion. He values love, relationships, and life. Those are only a few of the things God values, but these are also the characteristics of God. When we read about his nature and characteristics, we can only strive to be like him.

Tom Davis, in his book *Red Letters: Living a Faith that Bleeds*, shows how understanding who God is will transform our lives by how others see us.

> Learning to live a faith that is so real, you bleed Jesus. Here's how you start: Look for Jesus every

> morning in the eyes of the people you meet.
> And then look for him in the mirror.[77]

Our search for Jesus needs to begin well before we wake up in the morning. It needs to start the moment we take the time to learn who he is and what he values most in us and in his creation. Paul, in Ephesians 4:1–3, tells us that God calls us to run, not walk, on the road God called us to, so that we can be living examples of him. We can only do this, however, if we take the time to learn about him.

Identity Reversal

As we emerge with an understanding of who God is, we begin to go through an identity reversal. We begin to look up to God for an understanding of who we are instead of looking out into the world for acceptance and approval. We begin to make connections with the stories we read and experience emotions that link those stories of God to the stories of our life. We become folded into God's story by acting out our roles.

Our identity reversal can only come once we embrace the idea that the way we make decisions, and the source of our identity, has changed over the years. Instead of looking to our creator for guidance and our own outlooks of self, we have looked out into culture for identity. God's creation story tells us that we need to take part in a reverse engineering of our lives. We need to move towards and maintain a

---

[77] Davis, Tom. *Red Letters: Living a Faith that Bleeds* (Colorado Springs, CO: David C. Cook, 2007), p. 28.

lifestyle that says we are created in his image, not Zac Efron's. The Bible should be our source of inspiration and the source of truth—not MTV or Much Music. Do we base our wardrobe decisions on what we can afford, what looks best on our bodies, and is modest? Or do we base our wardrobes on what we see in the music videos, magazines, and billboards that surround us every day?

> God created human beings; he created them godlike, reflecting God's nature. He created them male and female. God blessed them: "Prosper! Reproduce! Fill Earth! Take charge! Be responsible for fish in the sea and birds in the air, for every living thing that moves on the face of Earth." (Genesis 1:27–28)

We are given a very distinct calling in Genesis to reflect God's nature. We talked about this earlier and it is extremely difficult to reflect this nature without changing the source of our identity. Mark Sayers takes the idea of reverse engineering our lives and gives a basis for change in his book, *The Vertical Self*:

> The horizontal self looks to others for a sense of identity rather than to something larger than oneself, thus finding a sense of self in one's status within society. With God playing no real authoritative role in informing identity, people look to others as the ultimate judge. Whereas the vertical self looks to heaven for favor and approval, the horizontal self looks to the world for approval and acceptance. For people who hold a

> horizontal sense of self, the creation and cultivation of a public image are paramount.[78]

It takes everything we have talked about so far to get to this point. Reading the Bible helps us to find the source of our identity. Understanding who God is and what God stands for allows us to see that his image is the one we should strive to reflect every day.

Reverse engineering our lives requires us to proclaim a few things that may be difficult for us to admit: He is big and we are not. He will be the ultimate judge, not Simon Cowell or anyone else. His ways are forever; the world's ways are temporary. We are okay with gratification that comes at a later date.

With the emergence of our new selves, we begin to live out our lives and stories within a new community. This new community is larger, more inviting, and more accepting because it is a community centered in God. This community evolves out of our Biblical worldview. In order to understand what a Biblical worldview looks like, we need to go all the way back to the line we drew earlier. Remember that?

---

[78] Sayers, Mark. *The Vertical Self* (Nashville, TN: Thomas Nelson, 2010), p. 17.

The question we have to ask ourselves now is, what makes our line right? Is your line more right than my line? Maybe not, but one thing *does* make us right. It is being a Christian, a follower of the way; it is asking, what does the Bible say? Anything beyond that is merely justification—when we try to justify the way we act, what we say, and what we do every day without looking to see what the Bible says. If we have a biblical worldview, we will have biblical values. When we have biblical values, we will have biblical actions. We have to focus on each one of those steps, because without one the others fall apart.

Let me give you an example. I was speaking in an East Coast hockey arena, a few thousand people all around me, when a guy walked up, saying, "Brett, I got it."

My response was, "What?"

"I got it," he repeated, as if I had not heard him the first time. He puts his hand out to shake mine, but as he does he drops a bag of weed into it.

I am instantly uncomfortable. A few thousand people at this point just witnessed a drug deal and I am the one holding the bag of weed.

I looked at the guy and said, "You are an idiot. We talked about this." He has a son at home who smokes a lot of weed and we have talked about it over a long period of time. His solution to his son smoking pot is to go home, kick down his son's door, and take whatever pot his son has and give it to the speaker. Somehow that becomes the end solution to him. He has done nothing to help his son.

"Where's your son?" I ask.

"What do you mean?"

"Where's your son?"

"I don't know."

"He's out buying more drugs right now."

It's not about the little bag of weed but rather the question, "Why?" Why is your son getting drunk? Why is your son getting high? The root of the problem is not the action. It is the worldview. The root is found when we address why he believes it is okay to smoke pot. The action is affected by the worldview. All kidding aside, the son was probably out buying more weed at that point because the root issue was not addressed. That is the problem we have with worldviews today. We look at our actions without asking why we do the things we do.

Dallas Willard, the author of *The Spirit of the Disciples*, tells us how we can gain biblical worldviews. "We can become like Christ by practicing the types of activities he engaged in."[79] This, however, is a process. Mastering these activities does not happen overnight, but we can start practicing to be like Christ right away. Our worldviews will probably align in some ways, but differ in other areas. Worldviews act like glasses or contact lenses, because it is essentially the way in which we view the world and its contents. It is what allows us to make decisions about our line as we ask what is an acceptable, Godly outlook on the world around us.

> When I fail to wear my God glasses, I'm left up to my own feelings and thoughts about faith, culture, and my role in both. With my glasses off, I can justify and rationalize sinful habits, sins, and philosophies that are a direct offense to God and His Word. However, the moment I start to filter life and culture through my own eyes is the moment I find myself on a path I don't care to be on.[80]

We would like to think we got it (our worldview) on our own, that we assembled and examined all the evidence and chose the worldview that was the most defensible or "right," then proceeded to use that worldview as our assumption for explaining things.

Sorry.

---

[79] Willard, Dallas. *The Spirit of the Disciplines* (San Francisco, CA: Harper & Row, 1988), p. xi.

[80] Oberbrunner, Kary. *The Journey Towards Relevence: Simple Steps for Transforming Your World* (Lake Mary, FL: Relevant Books, 2004), p. 125.

Most of us inherited our worldview. We got it from our family, friends, the media, and our experiences. Even Christians who claim to have gotten their worldview directly from Scripture probably didn't. More likely, we learned to approach Scripture with a worldview, thus even what we found in Scripture was influenced by what we expected to find. This "leads" our study of Scripture.

Paul warns us in Colossians that it is very easy for us to get caught up in a worldview that is based upon culture. *"See to it that no one takes you captive through hollow and deceptive philosophy, which depends on human tradition and the basic principles of this world rather than on Christ"* (Colossians 2:8).

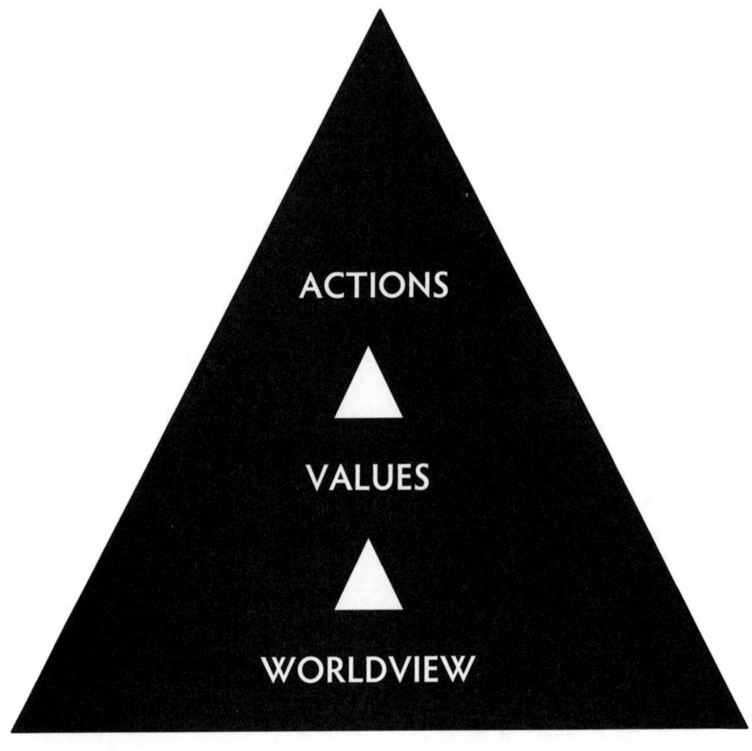

Our worldviews are integrated into our lives just like this pyramid. The young guy and his dad with the weed need to approach the problem in this order. Somewhere along the way, the son has gotten the message that smoking weed is either the cool thing to do, the solution to something, or he simply believes that it is the best choice for him. Where he got that message could be anywhere. It could be from friends, home, or through the messages found in some form of media. The son now thinks it is okay to smoke weed, so his values start to reflect that and then he acts upon those values and that worldview. The father, in order to fix this family issue, needs to address the root, which is where the son got the message that weed was a good option.

How do we prepare ourselves to be agents of transformation through our worldviews?

Community Living

The answer lies in community—not a community outside of culture, but a community that is engaged and participates within society and culture. A community based on the New Testament church, a church that is centered on the very essence of who God is.

Nate Larkin described this community in his book, *Samson and the Pirate Monks*. He bases community on three things: compassion, love, and helping hands.

> The church according to the New Testament is not a loose confederation of individuals. The

> church is a body—a living, breathing organism whose members are so intimately connected that they can only move together. On any given day, every member of that body needs help, and every member has some help to give.[81]

Our community, whether it is a church, friends, families, or simply the people we encounter every day in our local Starbucks, needs to become fluid, or even organic in nature. The values of Christ should flow out from us with ease and without hesitation. That is what an agent of transformation does best—allows their worldview to flow through them into the lives of those within their communities.

> The Christian movement must be the living breathing promise to live out the values of Christ—This is, to be a radical, troubling alternative to the power imbalance in the empire. In a world of greed and consumerism, the church ought to be a community of generosity and selflessness.[82]

The difficulty with reengineering our worldviews, our identity, and our need for true community lies in our feelings of insecurity. These insecurities may arise from making extreme changes in our lives. Moving beyond simply living in communities to being active participants and agents of

---

[81] Larkin, Nate. *Samson and the Pirate Monks: Calling Men to Authentic Brotherhood* (Nashville, TN: W Pub. Group, 2007), p. 73.
[82] Frost, Michael. *Exiles: Living Missionally in a Post-Christian Culture* (Peabody, MA: Hendrickson Publishers, 2006), p. 15.

transformation requires movement. Alan Hirsch, in *The Forgotten Ways*, concludes that, yes, movement and participation is difficult and full of insecurities—but this was, in fact, the way of the original Jesus revolution.

> That is not to say that every Christian literally left home and family to follow Jesus, but that the foundational spiritual transaction of laying down all in the name of Jesus was at the very base of all of their subsequent following. In this way they had made an abiding decision to enter into the liminality of leaving securities and comforts when they first became Christians and so didn't have to try and factor it in later. This meant that they remained a liquid people, consequently adapting and evolving, depending on context.[83]

What is the context of your community?

Is it family? Is it friends? Is it your workplace? Is it your local Starbucks?

Communities are wherever we go; they follow us because they are an extension of who we are and how we see the world. When we look to the Bible as our storyboard to discover who God is and then allow that information to change how we see the world and see what is right and true, God begins to flow out of us naturally to all those around us. That is the beauty of becoming an agent of transformation and the beauty of true community.

---

[83] Hirsch, Alan. *The Forgotten Ways: Reactiviating the Missional Church* (Grand Rapids, MI: Brazos Press, 2006), p. 241.

At this stage, story begins to penetrate our decisions and choices based upon our new worldview. This allows us to envision and live out our roles within creation. We join in as co-creators as we pray, socialize, serve, and are hospitable to those around us on a daily basis. We naturally begin to live like little Christs in our communities—and others take notice. They notice lives with meaning, happiness, and purpose—lives that are in communion with our creator and restorer. We become followers of Jesus!

What is a follower of Jesus?

> Followers of Jesus are people who are committed to partnering with God to make this world, the world that we all live in, the kind of place that God originally intended it to be. In Jesus' precise words, we're learning to love each other as we love ourselves.84

What message did Paul bring to these new followers of Jesus and their communities? Paul engaged them where they were—personally, emotionally, spiritually, and culturally. He went into their towns, synagogues, home churches, and places of communion and community involvement. Paul entered their coffee shops, homes, arenas, and church buildings as a means of establishing relationships and creating and fostering healthy worldviews with new followers of Christ. Even today, the best way to understand the communities we live in is to go where the people are. That way, you can see what values determine their actions.

[84] Bell, Rob. *Discussion Guide 001* (Grand Rapids, MI: Zondervan, 2009), p. 63.

Paul's opening addresses to each community in his letters allows us to see how community shapes and moulds us, but it is our communal worldviews that keep us connected with each other and with God's larger plan of restoration.

> Every time I think of you—and I think of you often!—I thank God for your lives of free and open access to God, given by Jesus. There's no end to what has happened in you—it's beyond speech, beyond knowledge. The evidence of Christ has been clearly verified in your lives.
>
> Just think—you don't need a thing, you've got it all! All God's gifts are right in front of you as you wait expectantly for our Master Jesus to arrive on the scene for the Finale. And not only that, but God himself is right alongside to keep you steady and on track until things are all wrapped up by Jesus. God, who got you started in this spiritual adventure, shares with us the life of his Son and our Master Jesus. He will never give up on you. Never forget that. (1 Corinthians 1:4–9)

> We're not in charge of how you live out the faith, looking over your shoulders, suspiciously critical. We're partners, working alongside you, joyfully expectant. I know that you stand by your own faith, not by ours. (2 Corinthians 1:24)

> I can't believe your fickleness—how easily you have turned traitor to him who called you by the grace of Christ by embracing a variant message! It is not a minor variation, you know; it is completely other, an alien message, a no-message, a

lie about God. Those who are provoking this agitation among you are turning the Message of Christ on its head. Let me be blunt: If one of us—even if an angel from heaven!—were to preach something other than what we preached originally, let him be cursed. I said it once; I'll say it again: If anyone, regardless of reputation or credentials, preaches something other than what you received originally, let him be cursed. (Galatians 1:6–10)

It's in Christ that you, once you heard the truth and believed it (this Message of your salvation), found yourselves home free—signed, sealed, and delivered by the Holy Spirit. This signet from God is the first installment on what's coming, a reminder that we'll get everything God has planned for us, a praising and glorious life. That's why, when I heard of the solid trust you have in the Master Jesus and your outpouring of love to all the Christians, I couldn't stop thanking God for you—every time I prayed, I'd think of you and give thanks… your eyes focused and clear, so that you can see exactly what it is he is calling you to do, grasp the immensity of this glorious way of life he has for Christians, oh, the utter extravagance of his work in us who trust him—endless energy, boundless strength! … He is in charge of it all, has the final word on everything. At the center of all this, Christ rules the church. The church, you see, is not peripheral to the world; the world is peripheral to the church. The church is Christ's body, in which he speaks and acts, by which he fills everything with his presence. (Ephesians 1:13–16, 18–19, 22–23)

I am so pleased that you have continued on in this with us, believing and proclaiming God's Message, from the day you heard it right up to the present. There has never been the slightest doubt in my mind that the God who started this great work in you would keep at it and bring it to a flourishing finish on the very day Christ Jesus appears… Learn to love appropriately. You need to use your head and test your feelings so that your love is sincere and intelligent, not sentimental gush. Live a lover's life, circumspect and exemplary, a life Jesus will be proud of: bountiful in fruits from the soul, making Jesus Christ attractive to all, getting everyone involved in the glory and praise of God… Meanwhile, live in such a way that you are a credit to the Message of Christ. Let nothing in your conduct hang on whether I come or not. Your conduct must be the same whether I show up to see things for myself or hear of it from a distance. Stand united, singular in vision, contending for people's trust in the Message, the good news, not flinching or dodging in the slightest before the opposition. Your courage and unity will show them what they're up against: defeat for them, victory for you—and both because of God. There's far more to this life than trusting in Christ. There's also suffering for him. And the suffering is as much a gift as the trusting. You're involved in the same kind of struggle you saw me go through, on which you are now getting an updated report in this letter. (Philippians 1:5–7, 9–12, 27–30)

You yourselves are a case study of what he does. At one time you all had your backs turned to

God, thinking rebellious thoughts of him, giving him trouble every chance you got. But now, by giving himself completely at the Cross, actually dying for you, Christ brought you over to God's side and put your lives together, whole and holy in his presence. You don't walk away from a gift like that! You stay grounded and steady in that bond of trust, constantly tuned in to the Message, careful not to be distracted or diverted. There is no other Message—just this one. Every creature under heaven gets this same Message. I, Paul, am a messenger of this Message… The mystery in a nutshell is just this: Christ is in you, therefore you can look forward to sharing in God's glory. It's that simple. That is the substance of our Message. We preach Christ, warning people not to add to the Message. We teach in a spirit of profound common sense so that we can bring each person to maturity. To be mature is to be basic. Christ! No more, no less. That's what I'm working so hard at day after day, year after year, doing my best with the energy God so generously gives me. (Colossians 1:22–24, 27–29)

You paid careful attention to the way we lived among you, and determined to live that way yourselves. In imitating us, you imitated the Master. Although great trouble accompanied the Word, you were able to take great joy from the Holy Spirit!—taking the trouble with the joy, the joy with the trouble… The news of your faith in God is out. We don't even have to say anything anymore—you're the message! People come up and tell us how you received us with open arms, how you deserted the dead idols of your old life so you could embrace and serve God, the true God. They marvel at how expectantly you await the arrival of his Son, whom he raised from the dead—Jesus, who rescued us from certain doom. (1 Thessalonians 1:5–7, 8–10)

If your life honors the name of Jesus, he will honor you. Grace is behind and through all of this, our God giving himself freely, the Master, Jesus Christ, giving himself freely. (2 Thessalonians 1:12)

The whole point of what we're urging is simply love—love uncontaminated by self-interest and counterfeit faith, a life open to God. Those who fail to keep to this point soon wander off into cul-de-sacs of gossip. They set themselves up as experts on religious issues, but haven't the remotest idea of what they're holding forth with such imposing eloquence. (1 Timothy 1:5–7)

So don't be embarrassed to speak up for our Master or for me, his prisoner. Take your share of suffering for the Message along with the rest of us. We can only keep on going, after all, by the power of God, who first saved us and then called us to this holy work. We had nothing to do with it. It was all his idea, a gift prepared for us in Jesus long before we knew anything about it. But we know it now. Since the appearance of our Savior, nothing could be plainer: death defeated, life vindicated in a steady blaze of light, all through the work of Jesus. (2 Timothy 8–10)

> It's important that a church leader, responsible for the affairs in God's house, be looked up to—not pushy, not short-tempered, not a drunk, not a bully, not money-hungry. He must welcome people, be helpful, wise, fair, reverent, have a good grip on himself, and have a good grip on the Message, knowing how to use the truth to either spur people on in knowledge or stop them in their tracks if they oppose it. For there are a lot of rebels out there, full of loose, confusing, and deceiving talk. Those who were brought up religious and ought to know better are the worst. They've got to be shut up. They're disrupting entire families with their teaching, and all for the sake of a fast buck... Everything is clean to the clean-minded; nothing is clean to dirty-minded unbelievers. They leave their dirty fingerprints on every thought and act. They say they know God, but their actions speak louder than their words. They're real creeps, disobedient good-for-nothings. (Titus 1:7–11, 15–16)

> I keep hearing of the love and faith you have for the Master Jesus, which brims over to other Christians. And I keep praying that this faith we hold in common keeps showing up in the good things we do, and that people recognize Christ in all of it. Friend, you have no idea how good your love makes me feel, doubly so when I see your hospitality to fellow believers. (Philemon 1:5–7)

Each time Paul came to a new location, he took the time to establish a relationship with the town's people. In each of his letters' opening lines, Paul establishes how the people's worldviews are influencing those around them. Those followers of Christ who are growing in the faith exhibit this in their actions and beliefs. Paul doesn't mention large church buildings, singular preachers, or great worship bands; he mentions their core actions and beliefs. The new Christian worldview changes the way people live, the way they act, and the way they are transforming the culture around them. It isn't always easy—and there isn't always a clear-cut plan—but God is changing the culture from the inside out.

It is time we start to think and act like the New Testament church. They started a revolution based on a new worldview. They stood out against what was the norm and said, "I want something more. I want a life that is everlasting."

Erwin McManus, in *The Barbarian Way*, explains quite simply why we need to become involved in communities at the most basic level, establishing the actions and beliefs of Christ as supreme.

> One of the tragedies of a civilized society is that no one wants to get involved. What becomes appropriate is to mind our own business. When we join a community that lacks a passionate heart for the world, we soon find ourselves acquiescing to apathy. It is a painful tragedy to see a brand-new follower of Christ alive with a barbarian spirit soon confirmed to the status quo.[85]

[85] McManus, Erwin Raphael. *The Barbarian Way: Unleash the Untamed Faith Within* (Nashville, TN: Nelson Books, 2005), p. 123.

Joining God in his restoration process is to live out a new worldview that mirrors Christ's values.

A New Worldview

Rob Bell says, in his *Trees* Nooma video, that we live between two trees. The two trees he is referring to are found in Genesis 2:9 and Revelation 22:2:

> Then God planted a garden in Eden, in the east. He put the Man he had just made in it. God made all kinds of trees grow from the ground, trees beautiful to look at and good to eat. The Tree-of-Life was in the middle of the garden, also the Tree-of-Knowledge-of-Good-and-Evil. (Genesis 2:9)
>
> It flowed from the Throne of God and the Lamb, right down the middle of the street. The Tree of Life was planted on each side of the River, producing twelve kinds of fruit, a ripe fruit each month. The leaves of the Tree are for healing the nations. (Revelation 22:2)

The question we then need to ask ourselves is, what does this mean for us and our calling to a new worldview?

The answer is found when we live like we have a God that is alive today. When we live out a worldview that mirrors Christ, we are living a proclamation that God is still active, God is still in control, and God still guides our lives each and every day.

> I need a God that is now. I need a God who teaches me how to live now. I need a faith that's about today, which helps me understand the world that I live in today, the world that you and I know is here and now, the place Earth that we call home. I need to know how to live here and find meaning and purpose today.[86]

Worldviews are interesting because they establish a life that is full of purpose. When we live with a purpose, it calls us into action, off the sidelines, and into a life working with God, promoting his values.

> We live between the trees in a world drenched in God. And some people seriously ask, "Where is God?" Maybe a better question would be, "Where isn't God?" I mean, his fingerprints are all over our world. Or maybe it's his world, and they're our fingerprints.[87]

Rob Bell asks some very important questions in that statement that I think we should all wrestle and challenge ourselves with. But I think there is a deeper, more important question that we need to ask ourselves: in what ways are we putting our fingerprints on his world?

The answer should come to us through a biblical worldview that establishes our actions, which in the end maintain and present our beliefs to the world.

We are given some clear examples throughout the Bible of how we can strengthen our faith, maintain our biblical

---

[86] Bell, Rob. *Discussion Guide 001* (Grand Rapids, MI: Zondervan, 2009), p. 62.
[87] Ibid.

worldview, and grow our personal relationship with God. These examples are called spiritual disciplines. Discipline is a good word for these practices and I won't sugar-coat it—they are difficult, just like any other life change we try to make. It takes time and energy to make significant changes in our lives, but by adding spiritual discipline we can grow closer to God.

Silence and Solitude

Silence is a temporary abstinence from speaking so that other spiritual goals can be attained. If you are like me, you wake up to music, take a couple steps into the shower, and turn on a radio. Then you walk downstairs and turn on phones, computers, and the TV. If you are like me, you medicate yourself all day with noise.

Why?

For many of us, this idea of being silent, on purpose, for any length of time, is frightening. When we turn off the noise, we have to deal with things like shame, loneliness, and the many shortcomings of life. It is a terrifying concept for us. Dallas Willard said in the book, *Spirit of the Disciplines*, that "silence is frightening because it strips us as nothing else does, throwing us upon the stark realities of our life."[88] In the silence, you cannot hide. We are confronted with our emptiness, loneliness, shortfalls, and regrets. So

[88] Willard, Dallas. *The Spirit of the Disciplines* (San Francisco, CA: Harper & Row, 1988), p. 163.

why would anyone want to spend time in silence if it leads us to confront these negative feelings?

The reason is simple. Jesus called us to fellowship, but how can we have a relationship with him if we don't spend time alone with him?

How does silence allow us to achieve other spiritual goals?

The time we spend in silence allows us to read clearly, speak openly, and listen attentively to the still, small quiet voice of God. It is through outward silence that we can begin to ask ourselves some very tough questions.

Do we fit God into our busy lives or do we expect him to find a place within our daily schedules?

Spending time in silence will in turn lead us into times of solitude. Finding silence and finding solitude are two complementary disciplines. Together, they allow us to spend some very important alone time with God. Solitude is the voluntary removal from all things public so that we can again, like with silence, be in God's presence. The hard part is finding a way to balance the busyness of our lives with our calling to create a relationship with God. "Without silence and solitude we're shallow, without fellowship we're stagnant. Balance requires them all."[89]

Time spent in silence and solitude creates within us an understanding of our true selves. It allows us to get in touch with our hearts, speak what is on our minds, and listen to the very plans God has for us. If we don't spend this time alone with God, our understanding of who we are becomes

---

[89] Whitney, Donald S. *Spiritual Disciplines for the Christian Life* (Colorado Springs, CO: NavPress, 1991), p. 184.

based on what the world tells us. Silence and solitude allows our understanding of who we are to be based on what God has created us to be.

Stephen Neil explains the connection between fellowship and solitude by saying,

> Modern man is a little afraid of being alone and of being still… Because we are afraid to know ourselves, we find difficulty in knowing one another. Because we do not know how to withdraw into ourselves, we find it hard fully to go out to other people.[90]

Our discomfort with silence and solitude is that their essence goes against everything the world tells us. Silence and solitude may not be the world's way of living, but they are Jesus' way.

Not sure that Jesus teaches this way? Check out these passages from his words:

> LAMENTATIONS 3:28–29, HABAKKUK 2:20, LUKE 6:12–13, JAMES 1:19, MATTHEW 4:1, PSALMS 46:10, MATTHEW 14:13, PSALMS 19:14, MATTHEW 14:23, JOB 2:13, GENESIS 24:63, MARK 6:31, MARK 1:34, PSALMS 62:1–2, 5–6, LUKE 1:20, GALATIANS 1:17, LUKE 5:16, ZECHARIAH 2:13, 1 KINGS 19:11–13, PSALMS 77:12, JOB 29:21, ZEPHANIAH 1:7, HABAKKUK 2:1, LUKE 4:42, AND ECCLESIASTES 3:7.

---

[90] Ford, Leighton. *Transforming Leadership: Jesus' Way of Creating Vision, Shaping Values & Empowering Change* (Downers Grove, IL: InterVarsity Press, 1991), p. 129.

In some instances, the Holy Spirit guides Jesus into times of solitude and silence so that the very worldly treasures that tempt us could tempt him. In Luke 4, we read that the Spirit guided Jesus out into the desert, where he was tempted by the devil. *"Now Jesus, full of the Holy Spirit, left the Jordan and was led by the Spirit into the wild"* (Luke 4:1). Jesus, at that very moment, had to wrestle with being alone and being offered the whole world. Jesus beat the temptation: *"Jesus returned to Galilee powerful in the Spirit. News that he was back spread through the countryside"* (Luke 4:14).

Many times, Scripture points out that through times of silence and solitude lives are transformed. Jesus understood that a balance was required between our busy, noisy, everyday lives and the stillness that silence and solitude brings. The question we always ask is, how far away from God can I get and still be a Christian? We should really be asking how and where we can listen to God and get closer. Jesus said it plain as day in Philippians 4:9: *"Whatever you have learned or received or heard from me, or seen in me—put into practice. And the God of peace will be with you"* (NIV).

Have a look at what the Old Testament teaches about the benefits of purposeful silence. 1 Kings 19:12–13 establishes that in silence we can hear from God. Elijah hears God not in the raging winds or violent earthquake but in a still, small voice:

> And after the earthquake a fire, but the Lord was not in the fire; and after the fire a sound of sheer silence. When Elijah heard it, he wrapped his face in his mantle and went out and stood at the entrance of the cave. Then there came a voice to

> him that said, "What are you doing here, Elijah?" (1 Kings 19:12–13, NRSV)

Where are you searching for God's guidance?

> God proves to be good to the man who passionately waits, to the woman who diligently seeks. It's a good thing to quietly hope, quietly hope for help from God. It's a good thing when you're young to stick it out through the hard times. When life is heavy and hard to take, go off by yourself. Enter the silence. (Lamentations 3:25–28)

Does patience come easily to you?

It is in the words of Habakkuk, the prophet, where we find the hardest concept for us to grasp when it comes to purposeful silence. Silence is used to worship God. *"But oh! God is in his holy Temple! Quiet everyone—a holy silence. Listen!"* (Habakkuk 2:20) I wonder if in silence, true silence, we hear from God because it is at that point where we shut out everything around us and hear only what he intends for us to hear. In that moment, are we like Elijah on the mountain as we hear only a still, small sound?

We have become so used to all the noise around us that we expect God to speak to us in the same way. We shout to get people's attention; it is how we rise up over all that is around us. When we become louder, we are looking to make a connection with someone who cannot hear us, but God works differently.

> There was silence before God spoke the world into existence, and silence for forty days before

> Jesus began His public ministry, which may indicate that silence is what allows us to speak as God intends.[91]

The words of Psalms 46:10 provide the connection point between our silence and our understanding of God. Silence becomes our link in establishing lines of communication with God.

> If I am not silent, and if I don't listen, how is Jesus going to give me rest? … Have you spent the same amount of time worrying and talking about your difficult, confusing situations as you have spent in silence, listening to what God might have to say?[92]

Silence is not just about receiving secret messages from God. It is about gaining truth and insights from the word of God. Charles R. Swindoll breaks down silence that way in his book, *So, You Want to Be Like Christ?*

> Yet somehow in the crucible of silence the Holy Spirit boils the truth we receive from Scripture down to its essence, reveals specific insights that are pertinent, and then applies them to our most perplexing problems and our most stubborn misconceptions. As He transforms our heart to

---

[91] Driscoll, Mark. "Silence," *The Resurgence*, http://theresurgence.com/silence (accessed March 8, 2010).

[92] *Nooma: 005 Noise*, DVD, 2003.

> beat more truly for Him, our decisions accomplish His will as we reflect His character.[93]

The companion to silence is solitude. They are companions because time spent in solitude, although frightening and nerve-wracking for most of us, provides key moments of reflection so that we can keep our worldview and God's word on the same page. However, getting time alone can be difficult, but let's take some more words from Charles Swindoll:

> Don't fight it. Don't rush it. And don't feel guilty. It's normal. Just let your mind run. Eventually, without trying and before you know it, your mind is still. Not empty; just quiet. And the things you have studied, the lessons you have learned, the scripture you have read or memorized, the prayers you have begun to pray will start to mingle and finally jell. The silly will be displaced by meaningful thoughts. Shallow will disappear as depth finds its way in.[94]

Solitude and silence bring us closer to God because it is in those times when we say "No" to distractions—whether it is TV, the Internet, friends, or even voices around us. We do, however, say "Yes" to his will and his word. God meets us in our silence and solitude and takes those fears of being alone and places them in his hands as he embraces us as friends.

---

[93] Swindoll, Charles R. *So, You Want to Be Like Christ?: Eight Essentials to Get You There* (Nashville, TN: W. Pub. Group, 2005), p. 63.

[94] Ibid., p. 71.

I often struggle with connecting my ancient faith with my modern world. That is a statement I find myself repeating every time I get up to speak to groups of people. Spiritual disciplines are an essential piece to the puzzle. Solitude and silence allow us to connect with God by making it easier for us to hear his voice, but sacrificial and simple living connects us to the very way Jesus lived.

We live in a culture of stuff. Quantity often takes the place of quality and we get caught up in the earthly desires all around us. God's word tells us over and over again that simple and sacrificial living is, in essence, living with compassion.

Simple and Sacrificial Living

Where is our heart? Is it in money? Clothes? CDs, DVDs, or MP3s?

Or is your heart focused on God?

"For where your treasure is, there your heart will be also" (Matthew 6:21, NIV).

Have you ever watched those new reality shows that deal with money and debt? The TV show *'Til Debt Do Us Part* is one of those shows. *Til Debt Do Us Part* follows financial guru Gail Vaz-Oxlade and her interactions with families as she tries to get to the root of their spending habits.

> Money is the number one cause of failed marriages. Rare is the couple that agrees on how the pot should be divided and the bills paid. Most

> families are in debt, and with debt come family arguments, tears, tantrums and marriages on the verge of divorce. To save families from the doldrums of debt...[95]

If I were to follow you around just like Gail does for a week, I would be able to tell you where your heart is.

God's word is full of warnings based on the love of money and earthly desires.

> Two-thirds of Jesus' parables spoke directly about money or passions. In the gospels, one of every ten verses addresses financial issues. In all of Scripture, over 2300 verses talk about money.[96]

Still not sure about what God tells us about simple and sacrificial living? Then check out these verses:

> DEUTERONOMY 8:18, JAMES 4:1–2, MATTHEW 10:21–27, MARK 4:18–19, PROVERBS 11:4, PSALMS 37:16, LUKE 6:30, PROVERBS 23:4–5, LEVITICUS 25:23, 1 TIMOTHY 6:8–10, ACTS 4:34–35, LUKE 16:19–31, LUKE 12:29–34, PROVERBS 30:8–9, PSALMS 37:7, PROVERBS 28:20, 1 JOHN 3:16–18, REVELATION 3:17–19, LUKE 12:47–48, MATTHEW 6:19–21, MATTHEW 6:33, 1 TIMOTHY 6:5, LUKE 14:33,

---

[95] Slice, "Til Debt Do Us Part," *Slice*, http://www.slice.ca/shows/showspage.aspx?title_id=93097 (accessed August 2, 2010).

[96] Groeschel, Craig. *Chazown: A Different Way to See Your Life* (Sisters, OR: Multnomah Publishers, 2006), p. 154.

> Ecclesiastes 5:10–15, 1 Timothy 6:17–19, Proverbs 3:9, Matthew 6:24, Psalms 49:16–19, Matthew 23:23, Acts 2:44–45, Hebrews 3:5, Luke 12:33–34, Philippians 4:11–13, Jeremiah 9:23–24, Job 31:24–25, Luke 16:9–11, 2 Corinthians 2:17, Luke 8:14, and 1 Thessalonians 2:5.

There is a great challenge in Richard Foster's book, *Freedom of Simplicity*. It goes like this: "Stop trying to impress people with your clothes and impress them with your life."[97] I think many of us fall into this trap.

Do we find it easier to talk to our friends about the new clothes we bought over the weekend than what we learned at church? Do we define ourselves more by the very brands we put on our backs than by our actions every day?

Our love of brands and possessions make true compassion very difficult.

> We can't reach far enough to offer compassion because our arms are too busy holding all what we own. If, on the other hand, we recognize that what we have is a gift, then we can extend our reach. We discover that we can use a portion of our gift to improve someone else's life, maybe even to save someone else's life.[98]

---

[97] Foster, Richard J. *Freedom of Simplicity* (San Francisco, CA: Harper San Francisco, 2005), p. 158.

[98] Davis, Tom. *Red Letters: Living a Faith that Bleeds* (Colorado Springs, CO: David C. Cook, 2007), p. 39.

This is a good start to figuring out our problem with simple and sacrificial giving, but I think it goes deeper than just having too much. I think it comes down to not having enough love and compassion. We have a hard time connecting with those who are hurting or have lost everything, because we are used to having all the "things" in our lives that make us feel secure. All the iPods, BlackBerrys, Starbucks, and having enough in our cupboards to last for months have taken away our ability to connect or feel compassion for those who are lacking. Feelings of entitlement have replaced feelings of compassion and we can no longer relate to those on the streets. We are so used to having everything that having nothing is something we cannot comprehend.

Have we become used to seeing people lying in the streets as we walk to school, work, or home?

Has it gotten to the point that the problem seems too big to fix?

If we are going to be Christ-like, should we not love our neighbour and be moved to show compassion for those who are cold and hungry? Is their pain not large enough to move us to action?

We won't understand simple, sacrificial giving until we start truly giving what we do not have.

How do we do that?

We start by giving beyond our surplus. What I mean by that is that we give not because we have some money left over at the end of the week—after we have bought everything else that we thought we needed. Mother Teresa said it best:

> I hope you are not giving only your surplus. You need to give what costs you, make a sacrifice, go without something you like, that your gift may have some value before God. Then you will be truly brothers and sisters to the poor who are deprived of even the things they need.[99]

Can you go without your tall soy latte everyday?

Do you really need McDonald's twice a week? However, it needs to go deeper. Simple, sacrificial giving is all about understanding and practicing compassion. It is impossible to separate Christ and compassion; they are seamlessly braided together.[100] Paul explains it very clearly in Philippians 3:10. To be like Christ, he says, is to want to transform our whole life to reflect him. *"I gave up all that inferior stuff so I could know Christ personally, experience his resurrection power, be a partner in his suffering, and go all the way with him to death itself."* Actually, all of Philippians 3 is about transforming our lives to be like Christ and continually striving to achieve it.

Did you catch the key to Paul's words? *"Be a partner in his suffering, and go all the way with him to death itself."* To be like Christ is to practice sacrificial living. Is that not what Jesus did on the cross? *"This is how much God loved the world: He gave his Son, his one and only Son. And this is why: so that no one need be destroyed; by believing in him, anyone can have a*

---

[99] Mother Teresa. *The Revolution: A Field Manual for Changing Your World* (Orlando, FL: Relevant Books, 2006), p. XIII.

[100] Rick Warren, Leadership Summit at Willow Creek Community Church in Chicago, August 2006.

whole and lasting life" (John 3:16). Paul tells us that this type of living is needed:

> Watch what God does, and then you do it, like children who learn proper behavior from their parents. Mostly what God does is love you. Keep company with him and learn a life of love. Observe how Christ loved us. His love was not cautious but extravagant. He didn't love in order to get something from us but to give everything of himself to us. Love like that. (Ephesians 5:1–2)

Sacrifice is a deep commitment to being like Christ. It screams out trust and love to our saviour. The definition of sacrifice is to give up something for the sake of something greater.

> Personal sacrifice begins with choice; who will we trust to meet our needs? We naturally serve what we trust. Hoarding wealth is a sure sign that a person trusts his things instead of his God.[101]

Let's go back to the verse in Matthew: *"For where your treasure is, there your heart will be also"* (Matthew 6:21, NIV).

Where is your heart?

Sometimes we don't give because we are stuck asking ourselves questions like, "How will I manage…?" When we are stuck on questions like this, are we really trusting God to provide for us? *"Look at the birds. They don't plant or harvest or store food in barns, for your heavenly Father feeds them.*

---

[101] Swindoll, Charles R. *So, You Want to Be Like Christ?: Eight Essentials to Get You There* (Nashville, TN: W. Pub. Group, 2005), p. 177.

And aren't you far more valuable to him than they are?" (Matthew 6:26, NLT)

The practice of simple, sacrificial living can start small—real small. Start by donating the coffee money you think you so desperately need to get through those long, cold February mornings. Those mornings may be cold for you, even though we have perfectly fine winter wear from North Face, but what about the morning for the homeless man lying on the corner who you pass every day on your way to school? Do you not think the morning is particularly cold and painful for them?

Here is a practical test in simple and sacrificial living.

Start with a blank piece of paper, like the one on the next page.

Now write out everything you have done with your money. Try looking back a year; that way, you will have a better understanding of where you have been placing your priorities. If you cannot remember back that far, I think the answer to where your money is going is—nowhere.

What does your list look like?

Okay, now take off everything on the list which you bought for your friends and family.

If I asked you to take away all the things you put on your list that were for you, would there be anything left?

Practical Test: Simple and Sacrificial

If simple, sacrificial living is living like Christ through loving actions and compassionate hearts towards others by giving up something for something greater, then the next step should not be too difficult. Having the ability to serve is a key step towards living like Christ. *"Whatever you do, whether in word or deed, do it all in the name of the Lord Jesus, giving thanks to God the Father through him"* (Colossians 3:17, NIV). Again, we need to notice that our actions, and how we live our everyday lives, are of key importance if we are to be agents of transformation in this world.

The following verses describe what should motivate us to serve. They provide examples of serving, as well as some application tips.

> HEBREWS 9:14, PSALMS 100:2, DEUTERONOMY 13:4, 1 SAMUEL 12:24, NEHEMIAH 2:2–6, ISAIAH 6:6–8, JOHN 13:12–16, PHILIPPIANS 2:3, GALATIANS 5:13, 2 CORINTHIANS 5:14–15, MARK 12:28–31, 1 CORINTHIANS 12:4,11, 1 PETER 4:10, EPHESIANS 4:12, ROMANS 1:1, COLOSSIANS 1:29, 1 CORINTHIANS 15:58, HEBREWS 6:10, JOSHUA 24:15, LUKE 22:27, MARK 9: 33–35, 1 JOHN 3:18, MATTHEW 20:20–28, PHILIPPIANS 2:5–11, ACTS 9:36, AND ROMANS 16:1.

Service

Christ describes the church as a body that needs to work together in order to make any change or growth possible. Without the cooperative nature of a group of individuals, life becomes like a three-legged race where we forcefully drag our partner towards the finish line with little success. Until we realize that we are not the center of the universe or the star of the story, or until we drop our pride, we will be unable to serve with a servant's heart.

> The church is not here for us. We are the church, and we are here for the world. When I ask church people to serve somewhere, I often receive a polite, "I'll pray about it, Pastor." (Which generally means, "Oh, crap. I don't want to do that, but I'll say something spiritual that may buy me time to plan my excuse.")[102]

I have worked with many youth pastors who have told me stories just like this. They tell me of 30-Hour Famine events where their youth have declined to fundraise or attend because they do not want to go thirty hours without food. The event, at that point, becomes all about them and how hungry they will be throughout the night. They forget something—that they are part of a larger story.

Louie Giglio, a terrific and gifted speaker, takes the time in the book, *I Know I Am Not But I Know I Am,* to describe what it means to admit that we are not the star of this story:

> But to mean it when I say that I want my life to count for His glory is to drive a stake through the heart of self—a painful and determined dying to me that must be a part of every day that I live…

---

[102] Groeschel, Graig. *Confessions of a Pastor* (Sisters , OR: Multnomah Publishers, 2006), p. 34.

> Humility, another word for knowing my name is I am not, can be described as "seeing God as He is." Pride is simply an admission that I haven't seen God at all.[103]

Service towards others requires pride to be placed in check, so that we can show and mirror the very life of Christ. Events like the 30-Hour Famine are not for ourselves; sure, they are fun and exciting times, but they are meant to benefit others. "The church does not exist for the benefit of its members. It exists to equip its members for the benefit of the world."[104] The famine event is just one example of ways in which we can benefit the world through our actions. It is a gruelling thirty hours because we are not used to being without food that long.

Can you imagine what it would be like to go three days without food?

That is only one question, but what about these questions from Bill Hybels in *Holy Disconnect*?

> What about the poor? Who will care for the sick and the dying? Will anyone visit the prisoners? Who will clothe the naked? Or take in orphans? Or listen to the hurting? Or give water to the thirsty, food to the hungry, and community to the outcast?[105]

---

[103] Giglio, Louie. *I Am Not, But I Know I Am* (Sisters, OR: Multnomah Publishers, 2005), pp. 128–129.
[104] McLaren, Brian. *A New Kind of Christian: A Tale of Two Friends on a Spiritual Journey* (San Francisco, CA: Jossey-Bass, 2001), p. 155.
[105] Hybels, Bill. *Holy Disconnect: Fueling the Fire that Ignites Personal Vision* (Grand Rapids , MI: Zondervan, 2007), p. 61.

What is that one thing in the world that when you think about it, it hurts? It wrecks you emotionally; it drives you to anger over the way things are. Take that one thing and strive to change it. Take that passion you feel and serve those who are stuck in those situations.

How many of you have been asked if the glass is half empty or half full? What if I told you there could be a third option?

> A pessimist, they say, sees a glass of water as being half-empty; and an optimist sees the glass as half-full. But a giving person sees a glass of water and starts looking for someone who might be thirsty.[106]

When we serve others, we are choosing to live out an active faith. A faith that shouts, "I will not sit back and accept a world that is out of whack." Dallas Willard, in *Spirits of Discipline*, explains the importance of serving as a retraction of negative qualities of life:

> I will often be able to serve another simply as an act of love and righteousness, without regard to how it may enhance my abilities to follow Christ. There certainly is nothing wrong with that, and it may, incidentally, strengthen me spiritually as well. But I may also serve another to train myself away from arrogance, possessiveness, envy, resentment, or covetousness. In that case, my ser-

[106] Gale, Donald. *The Revolution : A Field Manual for Changing Your World* (Orlando, FL: Relevant Books, 2006), p. 1.

> vice is undertaken as a discipline for the spiritual life.[107]

Service, at this point, moves beyond our pride and our love of watching life and not taking part. Serving others is a way to grow spiritually as we leave our pride behind and take steps towards embracing Christ-like qualities. When we make the choice to serve in Christ-like fashion, we do so with humility, because it is impossible to serve as Christ served without humility.

Worship

In the church, we are so blinded by the contemporary use of the term "worship." We take this term to literally mean nothing more than the corporate singing of praises to God.

What does worship mean to you?

A.W. Tozer describes the nature of worship as being a lifestyle and not an act at all:

> If you will not worship God seven days a week you do not worship him one day a week. Worship is not something that happens at a time and a place. Worship is a lifestyle that includes something that happens in a time and a place.[108]

---

[107] Willard, Dallas. *The Spirit of the Disciplines* (San Francisco, CA: Harper & Row, 1988), p. 182.

[108] Tozer, A.W. *The Tozer Pulpit*, Vol. 1 (Camp Hill, PA: Christian Publications, 1994), p. 51.

There are many ways to worship God once we understand that singing is not the end of it. Think about some of these examples:

1. Loving others.
2. Missions.
3. Spiritual zealousness.
4. Hospitality.
5. Acts of service.
6. Charity towards unbelievers.
7. Sacrifice.
8. Work, career, vocation.
9. Seeking justice.
10. Exercising spiritual gifts.
11. Not conforming to societal norms.
12. Singing worship songs.
13. Giving tithes and offerings.

Worship comes down to focusing our minds and hearts towards God. "To worship God is to ascribe the proper worth to God, to magnify His worthiness of praise, or better, to approach and address God as He is worthy."[109] True worship means that you have your mind, body, heart, and soul all focused on the greatness of God. To be that focused on something takes more than words; it takes a complete life to ascribe that much greatness to something.

One family that used their life and work to worship God was the Guinness family. Yes, that is Guinness like the

[109] Whitney, Donald S. *Spiritual Disciplines for the Christian Life* (Colorado Springs, CO: NavPress, 1991), p. 87

beer, and yes, they started brewing beer and creating a company that showed value in actions and words. Stephen Mansfield, in a biographical look at the Guinness brand and family, discovered it was the family's lifestyle towards social justice issues that made the company what it is today.

> What distinguishes his story is that he understood his success as forming a kind of mandate, a kind of calling to a purpose of God beyond just himself and his family to the broader good he could do in the world.[110]

Arthur Guinness built his company through focusing his mind and heart towards the people of Dublin. They (the Guinness men) also knew that what they had was a blessing from God.

> The continued good account of our Business calls for much thankfulness to Almighty God while we humbly ask for the infinitely higher blessings of His grace in the Lord Jesus Christ...111

The Guinness men of faith took what they were good at, what they trained and apprenticed each other to do, and concluded that their skills and talents could produce good in the world. They would go on to radically change the outlook of Dublin, especially for the workers at Guinness, but

---

[110] Mansfield, Stephen. *The Search for God and Guinness: A Biography of the Beer that Changed the World* (Nashville, TN: Thomas Nelson, 2009), p. 59.
[111] Ibid., p. 87.

they changed a whole city's future in the process. You see that, through the Guinness line, great men didn't just happen. They were given the support, trust, knowledge, and experience of the older generation so that they could excel and continue the good work God had blessed them with. They exemplified what many fathers today are attempting to do: teach their children quality lessons.

The only problem is that many times fathers today forget the key components: time and energy. The Guinness men had plenty of patience to pass on these traits. Worship for this family moved beyond singing and oozed out of their very lives. Everything they did emerged through an understanding of the blessing and grace God had given them. That is why the first aspect to "The Guinness Way" is discerning the ways of God for life and business.

> We know from his own words that the second Arthur asked these questions of his life and even those that followed him and who were not as passionate about their faith nevertheless tried to understand their lives in terms of a purpose God might be fulfilling in their time.[112]

We can learn many things from their story, but there is one driving force that we cannot overlook. They teach us how we can practically worship God every day. What do you worship God with? Your life!

The hard part for many of us is grasping this idea of worship going beyond singing. In churches all over the

---

[112] Ibid., p. 255.

world, as soon as the worship band gets up on the stage the rest of the church is asked to stand up and enter into a time of worship. However, many times the worship pastor is not the first person we see on a Sunday morning. Worship, to God, begins the moment we wake up. It continues as we eat breakfast, make our way to church, and enter the house of God. Just as worship begins before entering church, it does not end the moment we sit down and stop singing. It continues throughout Sunday morning into the prayers, through the reading of Scripture, moving into and beyond the words of the sermon and right into the fellowship we enjoy with our friends and church families after the service. Worshiping God is not twenty minutes of singing, one day per week; it is an all-day, everyday lifting up of our lives to our God.

That being said, if we cannot take the time to worship God one hour a week in community, how can we worship God privately seven days a week? Dick Staub writes, in *The Culturally Savvy Christian*, that worship and bowing down to God is an essential part of our ability to recognize that we need to step back from the conformities of this world and reconnect with the will of God.

> Privately, publicly, and communally, we practice the disciplines of Jesus to renew our minds, and as our minds are refreshed and restored, we find ourselves resisting the negative force of confor-

> mity to the world while experiencing the joy that comes through knowing and doing God's will.[113]

Think about Thomas' reaction when Jesus came to him and placed Thomas' hands in and on his wounds. Thomas responded by saying, *"My Master! My God!"* (John 20:28) At that moment, everything Thomas thought he knew about the world, death, and his worldview was crushed. He bowed down in amazement to what was before him by exclaiming that God is beyond everything in this world.

How often do you stop and exclaim, "My Master! My God!"—just like Thomas?

Chris Tomlin, one of the most recognizable figures in worship music, writes:

> It would be so much easier if Paul had used "songs" instead of "bodies." Or maybe "events" or "Sunday mornings" or… "Bodies" is such an encompassing word. This definition requires our mind, heart, soul and strength—our entire lives! And that's just what worship calls for, all of who we are. Any less would not be worship.[114]

The reference to Paul, in this instance, is found in Romans 12:

---

[113] Staub, Dick. *The Culturally Savvy Christian: A Manifesto for Deepening Faith and Enriching Popular Culture in an Age of Christianity-Lite* (San Francisco, CA: Jossey-Bass, 2007), pp. 107-108.

[114] Tomlin, Chris, "Articles: Whispers of Worship," *Royal York Baptist Church*, June 15, 2009, http://www.royalyorkbaptist.com/index.cfm?i=8011&mid=12&id=17017 (accessed March 10, 2010).

> So here's what I want you to do, God helping you: Take your everyday, ordinary life—your sleeping, eating, going-to-work, and walking-around life—and place it before God as an offering. Embracing what God does for you is the best thing you can do for him. (Romans 12:1)

Chris Tomlin ends his article by calling out a new generation, a generation that will take worship away from a solitary understanding of music into our all-around life.

> But I see new generations rising up with a burning flame inside to live out lives of surrender, of sacrifice, of worship to God. The Passion movement is a passage of scripture that best defines this abandon lifestyle. Isaiah 26:8 says, *"Yes, Lord walking in the ways of your truth, we wait eagerly for you; your name and renown are the desire of our souls."* This is not a one-stop deal, but a never-ending life theme, a life that stands in view of the mercy of God and echoes the psalm, *"better is one day in your courts than a thousand elsewhere; I would rather be a doorkeeper in the house of my God than dwell in the tents of the wicked."*[115]

Like I said earlier, what do you worship God with? Your life!

One of my favourite verses on worship is found in the book of Hebrews.

---

[115] Ibid.

> So let's do it—full of belief, confident that we're presentable inside and out. Let's keep a firm grip on the promises that keep us going. He always keeps his word. Let's see how inventive we can be in encouraging love and helping out, not avoiding worshiping together as some do but spurring each other on, especially as we see the big Day approaching. (Hebrews 10:22–25)

I like this verse for a couple of reasons. First, for its encouragement to worship together with others, and secondly, it asks us to look at why we are worshiping. Is it God we are worshiping, or are we just giving him lip service? In other words, are we worshiping only when we have to, or when we think others are watching? Maybe it is the other way around. Maybe we are not worshipping because others are watching us, making us feel uncomfortable. This feeling usually comes during moments of singing worship, but we can be encouraged that it is our heart, not our voice, that we worship God with.

Robin Mark, the composer of many worship songs (like "Days of Elijah," for example, and I strongly recommend looking up the lyrics), puts the heart of worship not in the words he writes but within the heart of the worshipper.

> No matter how foolish and simple our actions, if it flows on the fullness, truthfulness, sacrifice and passion of the worshipping heart, it will surely exceed the most complex and well-crafted praise symphony that man could ever create. It may even exceed the greatest sacrificial giving that man could make in life. It has **everything** to do

> with your **heart** and **little** to do with your **practice**![116]

Worship becomes all about our heart and mindset. Are we too focused on ourselves to worship God? Are we too focused on the people around us or how we are actually worshiping? God tells us that it is within our hearts and minds that we worship him, so the how-tos and the what-withs of worship become obsolete.

Have a look at some of the other verses that speak of worship. Read them and evaluate what they say. I hope you don't just read these verses and say, "Yep, it says to worship God." I would love for you to be able to read these words and ask yourself what God is saying to you about worshipping him. Maybe you are like me while I was growing up and did not like singing in public. It was because of that feeling that I struggled with the concept of worship and what it truly was. I didn't understand worship until I understood that it is our thoughts and hearts that are the centre of worship. Have a read through some of these scriptures:

> MATTHEW 4:10, PSALMS 95:6, MATTHEW 15:8–9, REVELATION 4, REVELATIONS 5:10–12, JOHN 4:23–24, JOHN 14:17, PSALMS 37:4, MARK 12:30, PSALMS 96:1–2, PSALMS 47:6, EPHESIANS 5:18–19, COLOSSIANS 3:16, ZEPHANIAH 3:17, MATTHEW 26:30, HEBREWS 2:12, PSALMS 22:22, PSALMS 147:1,

[116] Mark, Robin. *Warrior Poets of the 21st Century: A Biblical and Personal Journey in Worship* (Belfast: Ambassador-Emerald, Intl., 2007), p. 192. Emphasis mine.

> DEUTERONOMY 31:21, 1 SAMUEL 16:23, MATTHEW 11:17, PSALMS 33:2–3, PSALMS 81:2, PSALMS 150, LUKE 10:41–42, MATTHEW 18:20, MARK 7:6–7, ISAIAH 29:13, EXODUS 20:3, DEUTERONOMY 5:7, DEUTERONOMY 6:13, LUKE 4:8, ACTS 10:26, ACTS 14:15, COLOSSIANS 2:18, REVELATION 22:8, JEREMIAH 26:2, JOB 1:5, EZRA 3:10–13, PSALMS 29:2, PSALMS 42:4, ISAIAH 12:5–6, HOSEA 6:6, PHILIPPIANS 3:3, 1 PETER 2:5, AND REVELATIONS 19:10.

I will leave you with the words of Amos, a personal favourite of mine.

> At God's coming we face hard reality, not fantasy—
> a black cloud with no silver lining.
>
> I can't stand your religious meetings.
> I'm fed up with your conferences and conventions.
>
> I want nothing to do with your religion projects,
> your pretentious slogans and goals.
>
> I'm sick of your fund-raising schemes,
> your public relations and image making.
>
> I've had all I can take of your noisy ego-music.
> When was the last time you sang to me?
>
> Do you know what I want?

> I want justice—oceans of it.
> I want fairness—rivers of it.
> That's what I want. That's all I want.
>
> Didn't you, dear family of Israel, worship me faithfully for forty years in the wilderness, bringing the sacrifices and offerings I commanded? How is it you've stooped to dragging gimcrack statues of your so-called rulers around, hauling the cheap images of all your star-gods here and there? Since you like them so much, you can take them with you when I drive you into exile beyond Damascus. (Amos 5:20–27)

God does not want worship from us that is just lip service. He requires something far greater. The fact is, he does not just require true worship; he deserves it. He deserves our whole life, not just simple words that we read once a week.

What is true worship?

Your life!

Prayer

If we are truly to make a change in this world, we need to be able to communicate with the one who is guiding us. Prayer is just that—a connection with God. Prayer becomes our way to talk with God about our personal ups and downs as we experience them. Think about this: who do you trust the most in your life right now? It may be God, but it may also be your best friend, boy/girlfriend, parents, or sibling. Once you have identified that, ask yourself another question: why do you trust that person the most?

More than likely it is because that is the one person you have an open, two-way relationship with. They are probably the person you talk to most and the one you run and tell the moment that cute guy or girl asked you out. They are the one who spends time with you when the world comes crashing down around you.

God wants to be that person and we can communicate that openly and freely with him. The most effective way to do this is through our prayer life. The words Jesus spoke to us throughout the Bible are very clear about our prayer life and the benefits that come from having open communication with God. Have a look at these words from Luke's gospel:

> Here's what I'm saying:
> Ask and you'll get;
> Seek and you'll find;
> Knock and the door will open.
> (Luke 11:9)

Jesus tells us on more than one occasion that he expects us to pray and communicate with him. Prayer is an active communication that speaks of our trust in him. Matthew 6 gives us more direct words from Jesus about his expectations when it comes to prayer. If Jesus expects us to pray, why do so many of us struggle with doing it with regularity and humbleness? Perhaps we don't see our need for prayer because we have a high view of ourselves and a low view of

God.[117] Have we become so prideful that we think we are bigger than God? Do we rely solely on financial security in our lives? What happens when our pride gets us into trouble? What happens when our pockets run dry? God tells us what he expects us to do—pray. He is waiting to answer.

What should we pray about? How do we pray?

Here are two very important questions we often overlook due to their simplicity: Do you talk to your friends? How do you talk to them? The answer is simple. I know—you just do. There is your answer on how you pray—you just do.

Kary Oberbrunner, in *The Fine Line*, explains,

> Pray honestly. What's on your mind right now? Are you hurting? Tell God about it, and allow His presence to start the healing. Are you afraid? Unload on Him, and you'll feel a lot lighter. Are you battling with doubts? Dump them on God, and you'll be surprised at the peace. Do you feel like God isn't being fair? Tell Him. Don't hold back. He can handle it. God wants you to be truthful with Him. Let it rip. Give Him your whole heart.[118]

Do you talk to your friends everyday? I am going to guess the answer to that question is, "Of course." What about God? Do you speak to Him everyday? I am going to challenge you to something right now. I want you to

---

[117] Guinness, Os. *The Call: Finding and Fulfilling the Central Purpose of Your Life* (Nashville, TN: W Publishing Group, 1998), p. 106.
[118] Oberbrunner, Kary. *The Fine Line: Re-Envisioning the Gap Between Christ and Culture* (Grand Rapids, MI: Zondervan, 2008), p. 88.

memorize a verse from the Bible to help you remember to speak to God everyday. Are you ready? Here it is, from 1 Thessalonians 5:17—

> Pray continually. (NIV)

Pretty easy, eh? What can you pray about continually? Everything.

Try these:

- Pray for your pastors and youth leaders.
- Pray for each other.
- Pray for the billion people who at this moment do not have clean drinking water.
- Find a book on different countries and pick countries to pray for.
- Pray for the numerous wars that are happening around the world.
- Pray for the First Nations people in Canada.
- Pray for the single mothers in Canada.
- Pray that fathers will grow up and start being the godly men they are called to be.
- Pray for issues of justice (sex trafficking, water, AIDS, food, fair trade, child labour).
- Pray for the white elephant in the room—same-gender attraction.

That is just a small portion of my list, but my point is this—pray about what is important in your life. If it is important to us, it is important to God, and he would love to hear from us. That gives us everything we need to live out 1 Thessalonians 5:17 every day for the rest of our lives. That will keep us thanking God for who he is and what he has done. So, how do we pray? We pray.

Here are some key verses on prayer that can help answer some of the questions we have been working through:

> 1 Corinthians 14:15, Matthew 14:23, Acts 1:14, Ephesians 1:16, 1 Peter 3:7, Isaiah 38:2, Luke 17:1, Psalms 42:8, Acts 4:31, Philippians 1:4, Mark 14:39, Romans 1:10, Mark 9:29, Jeremiah 42:4, John 2:1, 1 Corinthians 7:5, Luke 2:37, 1 Thessalonians 5:17, Psalms 39:12, Psalms 88:2, Jeremiah 29:12, Matthew 5:44, Psalms 109:4, 1 Thessalonians 3:10, Mark 6:46, Luke 6:12, Acts 6:4, Daniel 6:11, Jude 1:20, Matthew 19:13, Mark 1:35, Psalms 66:19, Romans 12:12, Isaiah 37:15, Colossians 1:3, Psalms 102:17, Luke 11:2, Daniel 6:10, 1 Timothy 2:8, Jeremiah 29:7, Psalms 86:6, 1 Peter 3:12, Matthew 6:5–9, Matthew 21:13, Luke 5:16, Acts 9:40, Acts 13:3, Psalms 17:6, Hebrews 13:18, Hebrews 5:7, Revelation 8:4, Luke 1:13, Psalms 122:6, Mark 11:24, and James 5:15.

Fasting

What does it mean to fast?

The most common answer would probably be not eating for a prolonged period of time, but is that really what fasting means? Many of us, as soon as we hear the word fast, automatically think of events like the 30-Hour Famine, or giving up chocolate for Lent, but have we ever taken the time to hear what God tells us about true fasting? Read Isaiah 58.

> This is the kind of fast day I'm after: to break the chains of injustice, get rid of exploitation in the workplace, free the oppressed, cancel debts. What I'm interested in seeing you do is: sharing your food with the hungry, inviting the homeless poor into your homes, putting clothes on the shivering ill-clad, being available to your own families. Do this and the lights will turn on, and your lives will turn around at once. (Isaiah 58:6–7)

It sounds as if fasting in God's eyes goes well beyond not eating for a couple of days. When we read the words of Isaiah, fasting becomes less about abstinence from food and more about becoming closer to the will of God. When we enter into a time of fasting, we are choosing to put something aside to grow closer to God. So why do we not bless others with what we are abstaining from?

The Bible, however, only mentions food-type fasting. Mark Driscoll explains how fasting could be applied to other areas of our lives:

> Fasting is the voluntary act of abstaining from something for the purpose of growing in self-discipline, which is the essence of what it means to be a disciple of Jesus Christ. Perhaps the most common form of fasting is from food. This is because, as Paul says, for some people their stomach is their god. By fasting from food, they are learning to enjoy food as a gift from God without allowing it to become an idolatrous functional god that controls them.[119]

We need to start looking at the little things in our lives we take for granted which take over our lives. These things can affect many areas of our lives, especially when it comes to our media influences. In the same way Paul warns about gluttony when it comes to food, we need to look at how much influence we are giving to the media that enters our lives. Fasting, however, only works if it is a voluntary act.

If fasting is not a voluntary act, undertaken so that we can get closer to God, it becomes nothing more than the latest South Beach Diet.

> It is Christian, for fasting by a non-Christian obtains no eternal value because the Discipline's motives and purposes are to be God-centered. It is voluntary in that fasting is not to be coerced. Fasting is more than just the ultimate crash diet for the body; it is the abstinence from food for spiritual purposes… the voluntary denial of a

---

[119] Driscoll, Mark. "Spiritual Disciplines: Fasting," *The Resurgence*, http://theresurgence.com/Spiritual_Disciplines_Fasting (accessed June 6, 2010).

> normal function for the sake of intense spiritual activity.[120]

That is why fasting needs to be voluntary in order to be successful. It needs to bring us into spiritual growth and understanding, and only we can choose to do that. The best way to understand fasting is by reading about it, and the best place to read about it is the Bible. Jesus is very clear that he expects us to fast, just like he expects us to pray.

> When you practice some appetite-denying discipline to better concentrate on God, don't make a production out of it. It might turn you into a small-time celebrity but it won't make you a saint. If you 'go into training' inwardly, act normal outwardly. Shampoo and comb your hair, brush your teeth, wash your face. (Matthew 6:16–17)

In the same passage, Jesus tells us what to do and not do when it comes to fasting, but throughout the Bible we are given all types and lengths of fasting.

Matthew 4:2 and Luke 4:2 tell of Jesus entering into what we would recognize as a regular abstinence of food as he entered the dessert. He did drink water during this fast, though, unlike the fast in Ezra 10:6 which includes abstaining from water. Daniel entered into a partial fast of eating only vegetables (Daniel 1:12). There are even two instances in the Bible where fasting can only be done with the divine calling of God (Deuteronomy 9:9 and 1 Kings 19:8). Other

---

[120] Whitney, Donald S. *Spiritual Disciplines for the Christian Life* (Colorado Springs, CO: NavPress, 1991), p. 160.

than telling us that we must engage in fasting, the Bible does not tell us how to fast, or for how long we are to do it.

There are tons of verses that describe different types and lengths of fasts, because the how-long and what-we-fast-from is not the most important aspect to keep in mind. The importance is found in the outcome of our fast. Outcomes can include greater guidance from God, more concentrated prayer, a display of humbleness, delivery from the things that keep us from getting close to God, worshiping God… and those are only a few of the positive aspects that come from entering into periods of fasting. The fast is about God, not us. We need to leave our pride where we left our food—behind us.

Read some of these verses which teach about fasting. See how many variations of fasting there are.

> MATTHEW 3:4, ESTHER 4:16, ACTS 9:9, MATTHEW 6:16–18, JOEL 2:15–16, ACTS 13:2, 2 CHRONICLES 20:3, NEHEMIAH 9:1, JONAH 3:5–8, LEVITICUS 16:29–31, ZECHARIAH 8:19, LUKE 18:12, MATTHEW 9:14–15, JUDGES 20:26, 1 SAMUEL 7:6, 2 SAMUEL 1:12, 3:35, JEREMIAH 36:6, DANIEL 6:18–24, 1 SAMUEL 31:13, 2 SAMUEL 12:16–23, ACTS 27:33–34, DANIEL 10:3–13, 1 KINGS 19:8, LUKE 2:37, ACTS 13:2, ACTS 14:2–3, NEHEMIAH 1:4, EZRA 8:23, AND JOEL 2:12.

Study

Have you read your Bible from cover to cover?

Do you pick up your Bible on any other day besides Sunday?

If you answered "No," you would be just like 80% of the other Christians out there. That is why I talk and write about study. If you told me there was some faith group in the world in which only 80% read their holy book once a week, I would think it was a joke.

Wait a second… that's us.

Let me explain something about statistics for a minute. You can make statistics say anything you want; they present a bent line. You can bend and use them to prove any point you like. That being said, let's move past the 80% statistic. How often do you listen to music? How often do you go on your computer, play video games, or watch TV? If you said everyday, you are probably like me.

Now, how often do you read your Bible? Is it everyday? Is it as often as you watch TV or listen to music? The point is that if you are not reading your Bible, you have to ask yourself where your instructions for living life are coming from. Everybody needs to be reading their Bible everyday. A statistic on this matter should not exist because everyone should be doing it. Statistics are used to prove points, and I don't care what the stat is—whether it is 80% or 20%—because there is no reason we should not be engaging the Scriptures daily. I don't care what books you have read… you need to come back to the source. The source is the Scripture.

I was twenty-six when I first read the Bible cover to cover. I would read parts of it over and over again. We need to be reading the Bible on an ongoing basis as the church, as community, and as individuals. Rob Bell writes, "The Bible tells a story. A story that isn't over. A story that is still being told. A story that we have a part to play in."[121] If the Bible is this grand, overarching meta-narrative that we talked about earlier, would it not be important for us to read the Bible in order, front to back, at least once? I do not know too many experts on Shakespeare who pick and choose which sections of his plays to read. Especially before reading it in completion first.

How many Shakespeare plays have you read in school?

If it is more than the amount of times you have read your Bible, how then do we expect to live out the words of Jesus? We have to study the words of Jesus so that we can actively live out our roles in his grand story. First, however, we need to study the whole story.

How do you study the Bible?

You crack open the Bible and you read it. Did you know there is an app for that? Lots of them! Studying the Bible can be done anywhere, at any time, by anyone… as long as we are willing. There is also a wonderful website where you can read the Bible—www.youversion.com. On that website is a daily reading. I challenge everyone to get on that website and read it daily. YouVersion is striving to make our ancient faith and modern world connect with relevance through community reading.

---

[121] Bell, Rob. *Velvet Elvis: Repainting the Christian Faith* (Grand Rapids, MI: Zondervan, 2005), p. 66.

> We aren't just building a tool to impact the world using innovative technology. More importantly, we are engaging people into relationships with God as they discover the relevance the Bible has for their lives.[122]

Would it not be interesting if we got the churches we attend to read it together? YouVersion allows its users to choose different reading plans depending on their interests and how long they would like to participate, through customizable options. You can read the New Testament, Old Testament, single books, or even find reading plans centered around the chronological breakdown of events in the Bible.

> Have you ever wondered what it would have been like to read the Old Testament in ancient Israel? Or, the New Testament as the books were written? In this plan, the order of the Old Testament readings is very similar to Israel's Hebrew Bible, progressing from Law to Prophets to Writings. The New Testament ordering is based upon research regarding the order in which the books were authored. Although this research is not conclusive, it may offer helpful insights to your Bible reading.[123]

---

[122] YouVersion, "About," http://www.youversion.com/about (accessed August 10, 2010).

[123] YouVersion, "Reading Plans," http://www.youversion.com/reading-plans/all (accessed August 10, 2010).

YouVersion's simplistic and customizable options allow readers to engage the Bible where they are, whether it is at home, in the office, or on the go with their applications. Imagine if your whole church was reading the same passage together everyday—at their homes, on the subway, as families. Imagine the growth and conversations that would stem from that experience. We could say, "I am reading Ecclesiastes and so are you, and you, and you," and on and on it would go. At that point, we could say, "What is God saying to all of us?"

You might be asking yourself, "Why do we need to seek solitude, fast, or even pray? God knows I think about him."

That is true. God knows you think about him, but the question I would ask you is, how *often* do you think about him? All these disciplines are difficult and take time to fully master, but the Bible is very clear that God blesses us when we enter into times of spiritual growth. God becomes more than just a name, someone who we believe in when we enter into these practices. God becomes personal to each one of us as we trust him with the intimate details of our lives. When we pray, we trust him to hear us. When we fast, we trust he will be with us and give us strength. When we worship, we are showing him that he is worthy of our praise.

Think about this for a second. If you just met me and I told you I was a football player, after you got over meeting a professional athlete, you would probably ask me a variation of questions—like, "Where do you play?" If my response was an awkward and quiet, "I don't really play anywhere, unless you count my backyard," after you finished laughing you would probably say something along the lines of, "You are a liar." I wouldn't be much of a football player, would I? The same mentality can be taken when it comes to these practices as well. If we do not actively participate in a two-way relationship with God, in which we trust him completely, what kind of Christians are we? Are we just giving God lip service?

There are two questions we have to ask ourselves if all these practices are not part of our lives:

1. Do you know Jesus of Nazareth?
2. Do you know church, structure, and religion?

I could care less if anyone ever met church, structure, and religion. What do I mean by that? Well, I'll give you an example. One time I went to a church where I was the preacher for the night because the pastor was away. I came in and set up on my own, without anyone speaking to me. I sat in a pew off to the side and, again, no one talked to me. As we started singing songs of worship, I got a tap on the shoulder. I was thinking that a leader from the church was about to introduce himself to me, but I could not have been more wrong.

"Excuse me, son, you are in my pew."

I actually smiled, because that had never happened to me before, but I had heard about it, so I gave him his pew. The reality is that when our churches get full, each and every one of us needs to make sure that we are not turning away someone from outside our church. Instead, give them your seat. It is not about us. If these types of things do not start to matter, we need to ask ourselves, what do we really know? When we engage in an active faith, we can learn how to take our faith and transform the culture that surrounds us. Culture can only be transformed by active followers of Christ because our faith penetrates out from our actions and has a greater impact than mere words could ever have.

CULTURE

culture

What is our response to culture? What is our responsibility to culture? Well, the Bible talks about a lot of things. It talks about keys and locks. It talks about a small key opening a big door. It talks about leaven and loaves and how a little bit of leaven rises the loaf. It also talks about light and dark. People always say, "Light and darkness… right, I got this. I go to church."

Light Up the Darkness

Wait a second. Let's analyze this a little differently. If I took a Bic lighter and turned off all the lights in the room, you would say, "Light and dark… I get it. Now let's move on." What if I grabbed one of those eighteen million kilowatt bulb flashlights from Costco, the ones that do not even have a button—just a handle. To turn them on, you have to crack the handle down and a beam of light shoots out, making the Bic lighter look pathetic. That is the light we are after.

Is your life a Bic lighter or a beacon of light?

If I were to take that flashlight outside and turn it on, I would be grabbing a buddy and having *Star Wars* lightsaber duels right away. It shoots into the sky, becoming a piercing, blinding, transforming light. That is what we are called to be. If we walk outside with a Bic lighter, how many steps would it take before it disappears? Two? Step… step, gone? That is not the light we are called to be. Those lights are extinguished even before you step foot outside your door. How can you ever take your light beyond your front door?

Salt

My favourite analogy is salt. Salt is a preserving agent. In biblical times, you would not get your steaks from your local grocery store; you would get a chunk of meat and rub salt on it to season it. The salt would also stop it from going bad.

I love John Stott, the great evangelist, and I apologize because this is an extremely old school quote. Nonetheless, he says:

> Christian salt [you and me], has no business to remain snugly in elegant ecclesiastical salt cellars; our place is to be rubbed into the secular community, as salt is rubbed into meat, to stop it going bad. And when society does go bad, we Christians tend to throw up our hands in pious

> horror and reproach to the non-Christian world; but should we not rather reproach ourselves?[124]

The first part of that quote is basically saying: do not leave it on the shelf. *"And when society does goes bad, we Christians tend to throw up our hands in pious horror and reproach to the non-Christian world."* We blame society. However, we should be angry and full of reproach towards ourselves. One can hardly blame unsalted meat for going bad. There is nothing else it can do but go bad. The better question to ask is, where is the salt?

Where are we? I just do not think we are there.

Bob Briner, in the great book *Roaring Lambs*, says:

> Christians must penetrate areas of culture to have a preserving effect. And penetration does not mean standing outside and lobbing hand grenades of criticism over the wall. It is not about being reactionary and negative. It is about being inside through competence and talent.[125]

Us vs. Them

So here is the tough question. What makes *something* Christian and not *someone* Christian?

Why is Christian music one of the only genres of music on the planet categorized based on somebody's faith and not

---

[124] Stott, John. *The Message of the Sermon on the Mount* (Leicestershire: Inter-Varsity Press, 1985), p. 65. Emphasis mine.

[125] Briner, Bob. *Roaring Lambs: A Gentle Plan to Radically Change Your World* (Grand Rapids, MI: Zondervan Publishing House, 2000), p. 40.

the genre of music that they sing? I know bands that are Satanic and they are classified as rock. I know bands that are Wiccan and they are classified as punk. Have you ever noticed where we place an artist that is Christian on iTunes? They are labeled under "Inspirational." What does that even mean? When you look at the bottom of the iTunes Inspirational page, you can buy some Zen or Buddhist music. I don't know about you, but other artists inspire me at different points in my day, not to mention my life, depending on what I am going through. Should not they all be labeled inspirational? Why can I not buy my Jay-Z or Lights tracks on the same page where I buy my Chris Tomlin or Group 1 Crew tunes?

I was a teacher for over a decade and people knew I was a Christian because of how I lived, what I said, and what I did. If a band wants to go and leave our Christian world and sing, we have a name for them in mainstream media—they are called crossover artists. Where are they crossing over to? That's right, they are crossing over to where God calls us to be, but we as Christians use it as a negative thing. If I took all the plumbers from my community who knew Christ and created the Christian Plumbers of Greater Durham Region, you would think I was an idiot. Let them plumb where they plumb. Having a special classification for Christian music is a really dumb idea. It is a manmade creation from the mid-1970s, and to this day we still think it is biblical. But it is not.

We could make a Christian version of virtually anything. They have YouTube, and we have GodTube. They have Guitar Hero, and we have Guitar Praise. The world has Tic-Tacs, and we have Testamints. Then there is my favourite example of all—Twitter and Chirp. They are both bird sounds! We do not need to take something and make separate Christian versions.

What we are doing is not working.

Let's take Christian movies. I think Christian movies are really bad. Let's just leave it at that. Here is a paradigm change. If you are good at language and writing, go to a university with a great journalism program and get yourself a degree. When you graduate, go to Hollywood, Vancouver, or Toronto—wherever they are making movies—and become the head writer, who is a Christian, for *Transformers 3*. Then when someone around that table of writers says, "I have a great idea. Let's talk about masturbation again," you can say no and lean over and tell them to sit down. You are the head writer. Can you picture what the world would look like if a thousand writers, producers, and filmmakers who are Christians descended on Hollywood this year and the years that follow? The world would begin to change.

"Brett, I am not a writer."

That's okay. What are you good at? Use it to change the world. Last year, I was on a plane flying to Alberta and I noticed a guy across the way reading a Shane Claiborne book. In my head, I was thinking, *I know Shane*, and I start to talk to the man reading the book. I asked him his name and he told me it was Mike. I asked him what he did and he said he ran a hockey camp in Ottawa. I thought that was cool. He asked me my name and what I did, so the familiars were all out in the open now. We talked for a bit of the flight. We then got off the flight and were grabbing our luggage when this kid comes running up to him stammering, "M… M… Mike, I am a big fan. Can I have your autograph?"

"Dude, what's your last name?" I ask next. It was Mike Fisher from the Ottawa Senators. Here is a guy living out his life on the ice every night, changing his world. We need to start asking ourselves what we are good at and how we can live that out in the world—not the Christian world or the secular world, but simply the world. There is no sacred, secular divide. If you know Jesus, you are doing secular work no matter what.

How do we discern the culture we live in is a simple process. Start by looking at those top movies, songs, and video games we recorded earlier in the book and ask yourself a couple questions about them:

What is the worldview of the media? How does that compare with a Biblical worldview? What is my response?[126]

This will work with anything. What is Lil' Wayne's worldview when it comes to women? All you need to do is find any video he has ever done and you'll see what it is—you, as a woman, are good for nothing but sex. Then take that and ask, what does the Bible say? The Bible tells me that you are worth much more than that.

The response I would suggest is to choose your God. My pastor, Jon Thompson, has said, "Beneath all of our technology in Canada you will find the average person—educated or uneducated—involved in one or more practices

---

[126] CPYU.org with Walk Mueller.

that God says is nothing more than dangerous."[127] Jon then went on to name them off. "Tarot cards, psychic reading, crystals, the new age, witchcraft, horoscopes, outright Satanism, Ouija boards, reincarnation, séances, ghosts, levitation, palm reading, numerology, idols, astrology."[128]

Are these in our world?

My wife and I were shopping at Toys 'R' Us a while ago and my daughter, out of the corner of my eye, picks up this little pink case with a handle on it. I am thinking it is Monopoly Junior for girls. I look over and find that it is an Ouija board. It is at the Kraft Dinner height of any store. You know, that height where any little kid can see it and get excited over the packaging. What is the world saying when we are selling Ouija boards to kids? If there are angels and God, then there are demons and Satan. If you wilfully ask for a demonic presence in your life, I do not even have the time to walk through all the pain you are going to cause.

I go on to add some areas of concern to Jon's list. Sexual practices and sexual immorality (masturbation to porn, sexual movies, affairs). The love of watching extreme violence or torture. Downloading music, movies, or software. Abusing our bodies through drugs, alcohol, gluttony, and lack of exercise. Laziness, busyness, apathy, and lastly—not offering Jesus our sole allegiance but living a blended life.

There is no such thing as a biblical worldview in anything sexual. When we start living in this biblical worldview

---

[127] Tompson, Jon. "Sermon," in Carruthers Creek Community Church (Ajax, 2010).
[128] Ibid.

and lifestyle, we start to become like the conformists we talked about earlier. Our ancient faith starts to become clouded by the modern world as we allow our biblical values to be replaced. It is a biblical worldview, period. We are supposed to be pruning off those unbiblical branches every single day of our lives. It is a battle that will never end, and for some of us it is a battle that hasn't even started. If we are not attempting to win this battle, we do not have sole allegiance to God, but are instead living a blended life.

This is not the final word on the matter. Keep learning, keep searching, and keep reading. I think Yoda might have said it the best, and with the most clarity, when he said, "No. Try not. Do… or do not. There is no try."[129] We all have a choice. Choices to either live a biblical worldview that is in touch with our ancient faith, or a life that is of this world.

> Don't love the world's ways. Don't love the world's goods. Love of the world squeezes out love for the Father. Practically everything that goes on in the world—wanting your own way, wanting everything for yourself, wanting to appear important—has nothing to do with the Father. It just isolates you from him. The world and all its wanting, wanting, wanting is on the way out—but whoever does what God wants is set for eternity. (1 John 2:15–17)

[129] *Star Wars: Empire Strikes Back*. Directed by Irvin Kershner, Twentieth Century Fox Film Corporation (1980).

Dick Staub creates a mission statement for all culturally engaged Christians. He essentially lays out three elements of our lives that we need to examine if we are going to honestly look at media, faith, and culture.

> For we are called to be culturally savvy Christians, who are serious about faith, savvy about faith and culture, and skilled at fulfilling our calling to be a loving, transforming presence in the world.[130]

Is faith important to you?

Is it important enough to lead you to question your decisions about media?

If faith takes a backseat to culture, we are stuck in a biblical worldview mixed with… *(fill in the blank)*. That is not how we are called to live.

> Anyone who sets himself up as "religious" by talking a good game is self-deceived. This kind of religion is hot air and only hot air. Real religion, the kind that passes muster before God the Father, is this: Reach out to the homeless and loveless in their plight, and guard against corruption from the godless world. (James 1:26–27)

A fully alive life that is culturally relevant can only be attained with a serious grounding in the word of God.

Are we savvy with our faith?

---

[130] Staub, Dick. *The Culturally Savvy Christian: A Manifesto for Deepening Faith and Enriching Popular Culture in an Age of Christianity-Lite* (San Francisco, CA: Jossey-Bass, 2007), p. XV.

Savvy, by definition, is essentially having knowledge, being informed, and engaging whatever your area of specialty is. In order to have a biblical worldview and an understanding of your ancient faith, you need to achieve a balance of knowledge and application. Too much knowledge and we can become arrogant before the eyes of those we are trying to engage. When this happens, we begin to live like separatists too focused on the rights and wrongs of God's word, causing us to miss the true message behind his life. However, too much desire for worldly involvement leads us into the life of conformists. Being accepted by the world takes precedence over living a life for God. When we reach that balance of knowledge and application, we become true transformists. The world, and the people around us, takes notice of the life we live because it is not about us. It is about Jesus.

> You don't get wormy apples off a healthy tree, nor good apples off a diseased tree. The health of the apple tells the health of the tree. You must begin with your own life-giving lives. It's who you are, not what you say and do, that counts. Your true being brims over into true words and deeds. (Luke 6:43–45)

Do we know the skills needed to fulfill our purpose?

We are all on a journey. We will never know everything. That being said, our understanding of the third challenge lain before us is to stay informed. When we keep ourselves engaged, focused, and motivated, we can be a voice for those who are looking for help.

> So if you're serious about living this new resurrection life with Christ, act like it. Pursue the things over which Christ presides. Don't shuffle along, eyes to the ground, absorbed with the things right in front of you. Look up, and be alert to what is going on around Christ—that's where the action is. See things from his perspective. Your old life is dead. Your new life, which is your real life—even though invisible to spectators—is with Christ in God. He is your life... So, chosen by God for this new life of love, dress in the wardrobe God picked out for you: compassion, kindness, humility, quiet strength, discipline. Be even-tempered, content with second place, quick to forgive an offense. Forgive as quickly and completely as the Master forgave you. And regardless of what else you put on, wear love. It's your basic, all-purpose garment. Never be without it. (Colossians 3:1–3, 12–14)

It is there where we come all the way back to media, faith, and culture. Do you know what people say?

"Where do I start? Considering everything we talked about, where do I even begin?"

Engage Culture

Bill Hybels calls it your holy disconnect; you start with one thing. You start with that one thing that just ate at you as you read the book, the one thing that just wrecked your whole understanding of your life. Whatever wrecks you is what you start with. Maybe it is sexuality. You may be struggling with Internet pornography. You may be struggling with lust. Whatever it is, the first step is being honest with yourselves and those closest to you. Maybe you struggle with self-injury. You might be thinking of suicide daily. You may feel alone and abandoned, but reach out to those around you. The help and support you are looking for could be in the next room. It could be in the Bible on your shelf. You might be looking at your DVD collection and realize that violence has taken over your life.

Maybe the question is, do you know Jesus? Has the worldview of media replaced the God you used to know? I am encouraged by students on a nightly basis because you are the ones who care deeply about justice. You are the ones who are building wells, and I hope nothing stops you from seeking what you are passionate about. I challenge you that if an adult shoots down your idea, or dream, move on to the next one. If that fails, find another person and keep searching. We all look at life through jaded eyes at some point and it is about time we stop telling ourselves we cannot change the world and we got up off our couches and gave it a go.

You have three days. You have three days to make a choice whether what you read in this book is worth it or not. Do not tell me you will try. When you put this book down, when you go to your next movie, when you watch your next music video, or when you listen to your iPod next, you have some serious questions to ask. If after three days you have not started to ask yourself some serious questions, you never will, or at least not until you read these words again. That means all the time, all the energy, and all the thought that goes into a book like this becomes a waste of time. I challenge you not to make it a waste.

At one of my talks this year, I heard a young guy say to his buddies, "I hope he doesn't challenge my pop-cultureness." He was not willing to see past the Lil' Wayne or *The Hills* or the Drake worldview to the life worth living. He was stuck in this fake, materialistic world that had become comfortable. But I hope that is not you. I hope you start questioning everything around you like you never have before.

Media

I challenge you when it comes to media to discern it. Do not just buy into everything it says. Start questioning the worldview it promotes.

Faith

I challenge you to dive into your faith like you never have before.

Culture

How do we engage culture as individuals, in our families, and with our friends?

May God bless you with discomfort at easy answers, half-truths, and superficial relationships, so that you may look deep within your heart.

May God bless you with anger at injustice, oppression, and the exploitation of people, so that you may work for justice, freedom, and peace.

May God bless you with tears to shed for those who suffer from pain, rejection, starvation, and war, so that you may reach out your hand to comfort and turn their pain into joy.

And may God bless you with enough foolishness to believe that you can make a difference in this world, so that you can do what others claim cannot be done.[131]

---

[131] Groeschel, Craig. "May God Bless You With Discomfort: Franciscan Benediction," *Swerve*, September 17, 2007, http://swerve.lifechurch.tv/2007/09/17/may-god-bless-you-with-discomfort/ (accessed August 10, 2010).

contact me

If you have any questions or would like to talk more to me about anything said in this book you can find me through the contact information below

Email:

brett@brettullman.com

Web:

www.brettullman.com—my speaking site
www.yourstory.info—my self-injury site
www.worldsapart.org—network, empower, and support the Canadian church

Other:

facebook.com/brettullman
twitter.com/brettullman
youtube.com/brettu